The Stud(Ha.

MW01135986

Even with the highest-quality content, students who don't have an intrinsic motivation to learn may never perform to their full potential. So how can we create the classroom conditions where that motivation can flourish? Renowned educator Larry Ferlazzo has the answers in this comprehensive new resource.

Designed as a practical handbook you can easily refer to again and again for ideas, the book offers 50 teaching practices divided into four main sections: autonomy, competency, relatedness, and relevance. Throughout, there are tip boxes with links to resources for additional support, as well as lists of questions you can ask yourself to ensure you're implementing the strategies in a culturally responsive way.

With this book as your compass, you'll be able to create the conditions for students to find their inner motivation, be their true selves, and thrive in school and beyond.

Larry Ferlazzo teaches English, Social Studies and International Baccalaureate classes to English Language Learners and English-proficient students at Luther Burbank High School in Sacramento, California. He is the author or editor of 13 books for educators. He also writes a popular education blog at http://larryferlazzo.edublogs.org/ and a weekly teacher advice column for Education Week, and hosts a radio show on BAM! Education Radio. His columns on education policy frequently appear in *The Washington Post*.

Also Available from
Larry Ferlazzo
(www.routledge.com/k-12)

Helping Students Motivate Themselves: Practical
Answers to Classroom Challenges

Self-Driven Learning: Teaching Strategies
for Student Motivation

Building a Community of Self-Motivated
Learners: Strategies to Help Students Thrive
in School and Beyond

The Student Motivation Handbook

50 Ways to Boost an Intrinsic Desire to Learn

Larry Ferlazzo

Routledge
Taylor & Francis Group

NEW YORK AND LONDON

Designed cover image: © Getty Images

First published 2023
by Routledge
605 Third Avenue, New York, NY 10158

and by Routledge
4 Park Square, Milton Park, Abingdon, Oxon, OX14 4RN

Routledge is an imprint of the Taylor & Francis Group, an informa business

© 2023 Taylor & Francis

Library of Congress Cataloging-in-Publication Data
Names: Ferlazzo, Larry, author.
Title: The student motivation handbook : 50 ways to boost an
    intrinsic desire to learn / Larry Ferlazzo.
Description: New York, NY : Routledge, 2023. | Includes bibliographical
    references.
Identifiers: LCCN 2022044092 | ISBN 9781138631519 (paperback) |
    ISBN 9781138631502 (hardback) | ISBN 9781315208824 (ebook)
Subjects: LCSH: Motivation in education. | Effective teaching. |
    Classroom environment.
Classification: LCC LB1065 .F483 2023 | DDC 370.15/4—dc23/
    eng/20220921
LC record available at https://lccn.loc.gov/2022044092

ISBN: 978-1-138-63150-2 (hbk)
ISBN: 978-1-138-63151-9 (pbk)
ISBN: 978-1-315-20882-4 (ebk)

DOI: 10.4324/9781315208824

Typeset in Celeste and Optima
by Apex CoVantage, LLC

Access the Support Material: www.routledge.com/9781138631519

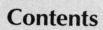

Contents

Quick Guide to the 50 Strategies

Chapter 5

Support Material

The figures in this book have a Support Material icon next to them, which signifies that they are also available on our website as free downloads.

To access the downloadable versions, please go to the book product page at www.routledge.com/9781138631519 and click on the link that says Support Material. You can then download and print the figures for classroom use.

The Support Material also includes a page with all of the EdTech Toolbox URLs as hyperlinks, so paperback readers can easily access the recommended articles.

Meet the Author

Larry Ferlazzo teaches English, Social Studies and International Baccalaureate classes to English Language Learners and English-proficient students at Luther Burbank High School in Sacramento, California.

He's written or edited twelve previous education-related books: *Helping Students Motivate Themselves: Practical Answers to Classroom Challenges*; *Self-Driven Learning: Teaching Strategies for Student Motivation*; *Building a Community of Self-Motivated Learners: Strategies to Help Students Thrive in School and Beyond*; *The ESL/ELL Teacher's Survival Guide* (with co-author Katie Hull Sypnieski); *The ESL/ELL Teacher's Survival Guide* (with co-author Katie Hull Sypnieski); *Navigating the Common Core with English Language Learners* (with co-author Katie Hull Sypnieski); *English Language Learners: Teaching Strategies that Work; Building Parent Engagement in Schools* (with co-author Lorie Hammond); *Classroom Management Q&As: Expert Strategies for Teaching; The Math Teacher's Toolbox; The Science Teacher's Toolbox;* and *The Social Studies Teacher's Toolbox*.

Larry has won several awards, including the Leadership for a Changing World Award from the

Ford Foundation, and was the Grand Prize Winner of the International Reading Association Award for Technology and Reading.

In addition to authoring a weekly teacher advice column titled Classroom Q&A at Education Week, he writes a popular education blog at http://larry ferlazzo.edublogs.org and hosts a podcast at BAM! Radio. His articles on education policy and classroom practice also regularly appear in the *Washington Post* and *ASCD Educational Leadership.*

Larry was a community organizer for nineteen years prior to becoming a public school teacher twenty-one years ago.

He's married, has three children and four grand-children, and is a regular, though mediocre, basket-ball and pickleball player.

Acknowledgements

Thank you to my family, especially to my wife, Jan. And a special thank you to Jim Peterson, the principal at our school, who has been extraordinarily supportive of me—and all teachers and students—over the years. I have to also appreciate the thousands of students who I have had the privilege of teaching and learning from because it's those experiences that inform the content of this book.

I'd like to also recognize three other people who helped make this book possible: Katie Hull Sypnieksi, who reviewed the manuscript even though it was going to be her summer off from working on books with me. Lauren Davis, my extraordinarily patient and supportive Routledge editor, and Jennifer Borgioli Binis from Schoolmarm Advisors, who made the writing of this book so much easier by formatting the manuscript so it was ready for submission.

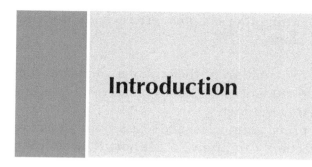

Introduction

Brazilian educator Paulo Freire has been a major influence in how many of us see ourselves as teachers. I often think of this comment by him:

> The teacher is of course an artist, but being an artist does not mean that he or she can make the profile, can shape the students. What the educator does in teaching is to make it possible for the students to become themselves.
>
> (Horton et al., 1990, p. 181)

Creating the classroom conditions where intrinsic motivation can flourish is one way teachers can emulate Freire's "job description" for educators, and I hope this book can be one resource that's able to help along the way.

It's designed to be a "handbook" that teachers can easily and quickly refer to for practical ideas that can help them at any time.

Chapter 1 serves as an introduction to the idea of intrinsic motivation.

Introduction

The remaining four chapters are each divided into similar sections:

- a brief explanation of that chapter's concept that can help students motivate themselves, including supporting research;
- instructional strategies and classroom practices that teachers can apply to support that concept, including online links to additional support; and
- questions teachers can ask themselves to ensure that they are implementing the strategies in a way that is culturally responsive.

I hope readers will find these ideas useful and will feel free to modify and adapt them.

Please look at this book as a compass, and not necessarily as a road map, to guide all of us as we "try to make it possible for the students to become themselves."

Note: All figures in the book are available to be freely downloaded at the Routledge website.

Reference

Horton, M., Bell, B., Gaventa, J., & Peters, J. M. (1990). *We make the road by walking: Conversations on education and social change.* Temple University Press.

1 Motivation in the Classroom

A case can be made, and researchers have made it, that motivation is one of the keystones of teaching and learning (Dorn et al., 2017).

As an educator, based on my life and professional experience, I may have a fairly solid idea of what I believe students might need to know in order to be successful academically and professionally. However, how much does that matter if my students are not motivated to learn what I am teaching?

Of course, I can try to entice their interest through "dangling carrots" like grades, points, prizes, gold stars, etc. (or threatening "sticks" like detention or negative calls home). This kind of "extrinsic motivation" can work, but usually only for the short term and typically for tasks that don't require much higher-order thinking (Farnam Street, n.d.).

On the other hand, "intrinsic motivation" describes a situation where the energy to act comes more from inside the learner. In other words, the reward is the activity itself. The late educator Ken Robinson talked (Ferlazzo, 2012) about how farmers can't force their crops to grow, but they can create the conditions that support their seeds' ability to grow—providing the right soil, water, and care. This description is similar

DOI: 10.4324/9781315208824-1

1

to the challenge teachers face with encouraging student intrinsic motivation—we can't *make* them have it, but we can create the classroom conditions where that kind of motivation is more likely to develop and flourish.

Extensive research documents the benefits of intrinsic motivation over the extrinsic kind. Intrinsic motivation tends to lead to greater academic achievement and a better sense of well-being (Burton et al., 2006) lasts longer, enhances creativity, and cultivates higher-order thinking (Brewster & Fager, 2000).

Extrinsic motivation tends to reduce long-term interest and effort in the topic at hand (Deci et al., 1999; Kohn, 2018; Wehe et al., 2015) and reduce creativity, as well (Hennessey, 2000). Research has found that motivation driven by extrinsic factors tends to lead to "decreased well-being" (Howard et al., 2021). Experiments using student rewards to improve academic achievement have failed repeatedly (Adams, 2014; Dietrichson et al., 2020; Ferlazzo, 2016). If and when incentives have resulted in very limited short-term "success," researchers have found they tend to increase participants' focus on the reward itself, not on the task. Work quality then suffers, and task interest tends to decline to previous levels—or below them—after the reward is given (Kohn, 2016).

Students, especially teens, in the United States report exceptionally high feelings of disengagement from school (Sparks, 2020; Yale University, 2020)—and that was before the COVID pandemic. It does not seem to be a stretch to consider that the high levels of extrinsic motivation present in most classes and schools might contribute to these strong negative perspectives.

Emphasizing intrinsic motivation also makes me feel better about myself as a teacher and, I believe, also contributes towards creating an overall class atmosphere of a "community of learners" instead of a "classroom of students." No one wants to be treated like a rat in a maze, and I certainly don't want to view myself as a teacher who even vaguely can be described as promoting that kind of system.

Does that mean I never use extrinsic motivation in my classroom? Of course not. I was a community organizer for nineteen years prior to becoming a secondary teacher twenty years ago. Organizers talk about working "in the world as it is" and not in "the world as we'd like it to be." Creating the conditions to encourage student intrinsic motivation can sometimes be hard and time-consuming. It's not at all unusual for me to offer extra credit, grade by using points, and offer healthy snacks as game prizes, and I am definitely not above sometimes "threatening" negative consequences for inappropriate behaviors. I am not a Pollyanna with my head up in the clouds, and live "in the world as it is." However, often (though not always) when I apply "carrots," I also briefly talk with students about how it is more of an exception to the "rule." The "rule" is that I hope students generally do things in our class because they want to, and not because they feel a need to pursue rewards.

When it comes to using "sticks," I try to follow the advice (with a slight adjustment) of Dr. Edward Deci, perhaps the preeminent researcher in the world on intrinsic motivation. He acknowledges that a negative consequence might have to be used but, then "You need to sit down the next afternoon when everyone's calm, talk it through from both sides, then discuss ways so the behavior doesn't happen again . . . Always use the blow-up as a learning moment the next day" (Feiler, 2013, para. 18). My modification to his advice comes from my community organizing experience, where we learned that "polarization" can happen, but that "depolarization" can be most effective if it happens fairly quickly. In that spirit, I try to make that follow-up conversation happen during the same class or track the student down later in the day.

It is also important to keep in mind that students—and the rest of us—can be motivated by both a desire to learn what is being taught and wanting a good grade, just as an interest in being a better teacher motivated me to write this book, as well as the possible additional income I could gain from royalties.

Let's also recognize the role of what writer Daniel Pink calls "baseline rewards" (Farnam Street, n.d.) and that is also supported by other research (Ferlazzo, 2015; Kaplan, 2015). The "baseline rewards" concept suggests that basic extrinsic "rewards" in a classroom (a caring teacher, engaging lessons, predictable and fair grading, cleanliness, respectful rules and atmosphere, etc.) or in a job situation (reasonable salary, safe working conditions) must be present for people to have any sort of motivation at all. Absent those kinds of "baseline rewards" and participants will tend to focus on the inequitable and unfair situation rather than on learning or on being productive.

But even though I recognize the role of extrinsic motivation in the lives of my students and in my life, I am also constantly striving in my classroom to create "the world as I'd like it to be" by creating the conditions where intrinsic motivation can blossom. This book shares what teachers can do to make that world happen more often in our classes.

For effective educators, there is always tension between "the world as it is" and "the world as we'd like it to be." If we always operate out of the former, we can become transactional pragmatists always settling for what appears to be the easiest short-term solution. If we always operate out of the latter, we can become hopeless sentimentalists who are likely to become disillusioned and burnt-out. But it's not a question of either/or and, instead, it's more of one considering which side do you tend to operate on, and if you tend to use the former to lead you to more of the latter. I would suggest that favoring that side of the coin is the perspective that is more likely to keep you—and your students—in a content and effective learning situation.

Researchers have identified four general areas that can contribute towards creating the conditions where intrinsic motivation can be supported (Center on Education Policy, 2012; Ryan & Deci, 2000), and they serve as the basis for the next four chapters in this book:

1. Autonomy: having a degree of control over what needs to happen and how it can be done.
2. Competence: feeling that one has the ability to be successful in doing it.
3. Relatedness: doing the activity helps the student feel more connected to others, and feel cared about by people whom they respect.
4. Relevance: the work must be seen by students as interesting and valuable to them, and useful to their present lives and/or hopes and dreams for the future.

Not everything we do in the classroom has to involve all four of these elements, but I do think we can include some of them in most of our lessons. There will be times, however, that students are required to do tasks that make it challenging to include even one of them (for example, taking state standardized tests). In those cases, I believe it's a safe guess that students are likely to be more engaged in them if their teachers have emphasized the conditions for intrinsic motivation most of the rest of the time.

Apart from the many specific activities described in this book, we teachers can also be challenged to have what could be called an "Intrinsic Motivation Mindset." Each day, we will have many "small" opportunities not mentioned in this book to promote these four elements. Perhaps we can promote autonomy by giving students the option of completing an assignment online or on paper. Or perhaps we can make a slight adjustment to our lesson plan one day to incorporate something about a major news event that just occurred. In the midst of all the pressures we face day-in-and-day-out, the more we can train ourselves to make this kind of mindset part of our routine, the more engaged our students will be and we, in turn, can gain energy from that kind of positive reinforcement.

All the strategies as described in this book can be effective with most students. However, they can be more effective if we also look at them through a culturally responsive lens that we are always wearing. The majority of students in public schools are students of color, while the majority of teachers are white. Ignoring the fact that many of us have had, and continue to have, different cultural and life experiences from our students is not a wise professional practice.

Though we all have control over how we act and react in situations, we don't always have control over all the factors that have led us into those situations. This is especially true for many of our students who come from economically challenged backgrounds. Research has found that students from low-income families understandably tend to feel like they have less power and agency in their lives than those students from more economically secure families (Shifrer, 2019).

The strategies in this book offer one way to possibly begin to at least slightly change that dynamic. Though culturally responsive ideas can be found throughout each section, the end of each chapter contains questions that teachers might consider asking themselves to ensure that they infuse cultural responsiveness as they implement these intrinsic motivation strategies. Without doing so could be the equivalent of saying the words without playing the music. Cultural responsiveness is not an "add-on," it is a core teacher competency.

Using these ideas to help our students develop intrinsic motivation, and applying them through a culturally responsive lens, can have major positive impacts on our students. However, they should not be viewed as the answer to the real problems facing many of them—researchers have concluded that as much as two-thirds of the factors that influence academic achievement lay outside the schoolhouse walls in equity issues like income inequality and systemic racism (Ferlazzo, 2010; Rothstein, 2010).

Perhaps some of these teaching and learning strategies might also better prepare them—and us—to work to change some of those outside factors. By doing so, we might be able to make the world a better place for our students, their families, and for us.

EDTECH TOOLBOX

My friend, colleague and often co-author Katie Hull Sypnieski and I worked with Education Week to create four short, animated videos on the four elements required to support intrinsic motivation: Autonomy, Competence, Relatedness and Relevance. They serve as good introductions to these ideas. They are freely available at "Here Are Our Four New Ed Week Videos on Student Motivation!" (https://larryferlazzo.edublogs.org/2019/12/09/here-are-our-four-new-ed-week-videos-on-student-motivation/).

References

Adams, R. (2014, October 3). Student rewards such as cash and free trips fail to improve GCSE results. www.theguardian.com/education/2014/oct/03/student-rewards-cash-free-trips-fail-improve-gcse-results

Brewster, C., & Fager, J. (2000). *Increasing student engagement and motivation: From time-on-task to homework*. Northwest Regional Educational Laboratory. https://educationnorthwest.org/sites/default/files/byrequest.pdf

Burton, K. D., Lydon, J. E., D'Alessandro, D. U., & Koestner, R. (2006). The differential effects of intrinsic and identified motivation on well-being and performance: Prospective, experimental, and implicit approaches to self-determination theory. *Journal of Personality and Social Psychology, 91*(4), 750–762. https://doi.org/10.1037/0022-3514.91.4.750

Center on Education Policy. (2012). *What is motivation and why does it matter?* The George Washington University. https://files.eric.ed.gov/fulltext/ED532670.pdf

Deci, E. L., Koestner, R., & Ryan, R. M. (1999). A meta-analytic review of experiments examining the effects of extrinsic rewards on intrinsic motivation. *Psychological Bulletin, 125*(6), 627–668. https://doi.org/10.1037/0033-2909.125.6.627

Dietrichson, J., Filges, T., Klokker, R. H., Viinholt, B. C. A., Bøg, M., & Jensen, U. H. (2020). Targeted school-based interventions for improving reading and mathematics for students with, or at risk of, academic difficulties in Grades 7–12: A systematic review. *Campbell Systematic Reviews, 16*(2). https://doi.org/10.1002/cl2.1081

Dorn, E., Krawitz, M., & Mourshed, M. (2017). How to improve student educational outcomes: New insights from data analytics. www.mckinsey.com/industries/education/our-insights/how-to-improve-student-educational-outcomes-new-insights-from-data-analytics

Farnam Street. (n.d.). Daniel Pink on incentives and the two types of motivation. https://fs.blog/daniel-pink-two-types-of-motivation/

Feiler, B. (2013, January 11). Train a parent, spare a child. *The New York Times.* www.nytimes.com/2013/01/13/fashion/modifying-a-childs-behavior-without-resorting-to-bribes-this-life.html

Ferlazzo, L. (2010, December 28). The best places to learn what impact a teacher & outside factors have on student achievement. *Larry Ferlazzo's Website of the Day.* https://larryferlazzo.edublogs.org/2010/12/28/the-best-places-to-learn-what-impact-a-teacher-outside-factors-have-on-student-achievement/

Ferlazzo, L. (2012, June 4). "You cannot make a plant grow—You can provide the conditions for growth." *Larry Ferlazzo's Website of the Day.* https://larryferlazzo.edublogs.org/2012/06/04/you-cannot-make-a-plant-grow-you-can-provide-the-conditions-for-growth/

Ferlazzo, L. (2015, August 8). Quote of the day: What helps & hurts motivation? *Larry Ferlazzo's Website of the Day.* https://larryferlazzo.edublogs.org/2015/08/08/quote-of-the-day-what-helps-hurts-motivation

Ferlazzo, L. (2016, May 18). The incentive follies. *Larry Ferlazzo's Website of the Day.* https://larryferlazzo.edublogs.org/2016/05/18/the-incentive-follies/

Ferlazzo, L. (2019, December 9). Here are our four new ed week videos on student motivation. *Larry Ferlazzo's Website of the Day.* https://larryferlazzo.edublogs.org/2019/12/09/here-are-our-four-new-ed-week-videos-on-student-motivation/.

Hennessey, B. A. (2000). Rewards and creativity. In *Intrinsic and extrinsic motivation* (pp. 55–78). Elsevier. https://doi.org/10.1016/B978-012619070-0/50025-8

Howard, J. L., Bureau, J., Guay, F., Chong, J. X. Y., & Ryan, R. M. (2021). Student motivation and associated outcomes: A meta-analysis from self-determination theory. *Perspectives on Psychological Science, 16*(6), 1300–1323. https://doi.org/10.1177/1745691620966789

Kaplan, J. (2015, August 7). It pays to give thanks at the office. *The Wall Street Journal.* www.wsj.com/articles/it-pays-to-give-thanks-at-the-office-14389 59788

Kohn, A. (2016, October 5). Why dangling rewards in front of students and teachers is counterproductive. *The Washington Post.* www.washingtonpost.com/news/answer-sheet/wp/2016/10/05/why-dangling-rewards-in-front-of-students-and-teachers-is-counter productive/

Kohn, A. (2018, October 27). Science confirms it: People are not pets. *The New York Times.* www.nytimes.com/2018/10/27/opinion/sunday/science-rewards-behavior.html

Rothstein, R. (2010). *How to fix our schools* (No. 286). Economic Policy Institute. https://files.epi.org/page/-/pdf/ib286.pdf

Ryan, R. M., & Deci, E. L. (2000). Intrinsic and Extrinsic Motivations: Classic Definitions and New Directions. *Contemporary Educational Psychology, 25*(1), 54–67. https://doi.org/10.1006/ceps.1999.1020

Shifrer, D. (2019). The contributions of parental, academic, school, and peer factors to differences by socioeconomic status in adolescents' locus of control. *Society and Mental Health, 9*(1), 74–94. https://doi.org/10.1177/2156869318754321

Sparks, S. D. (2020, June 22). Part of global trend, 1 in 3 US high schoolers felt disconnected from school before pandemic. *Education Week.* www.edweek.org/policy-politics/part-of-global-trend-1-in-3-u-s-high-schoolers-felt-disconnected-from-school-before-pandemic/2020/06

Wehe, H. S., Rhodes, M. G., & Seger, C. A. (2015). Evidence for the negative impact of reward on self-regulated learning. *Quarterly Journal of Experimental*

Psychology, 68(11), 2125–2130. https://doi.org/10.1080/ 17470218.2015.1061566

Yale University. (2020, January 30). Students' feelings about high school are mostly negative. *ScienceDaily.* www.sciencedaily.com/releases/2020/01/20013017 3558.htm

2 | What Is "Autonomy" and Why Is it Important?

Autonomy means having some control over what you do and how you can do it, and extensive research has found that providing students with choices promotes a sense of autonomy and intrinsic motivation (NASEM et al., 2018). But it is not simply a matter of students just having options—offering students the choice of which side of the paper they write their essay on does not promote a sense of autonomy!

In order to promote the development of intrinsic motivation, the options must also have some connection to student interest (Katz & Assor, 2007). This point clarifies that the four elements supporting the development of intrinsic motivation, though useful categories for exploration, are not entirely separate "silos." All are interconnected as, in this case, "relevance" is a critical part of supporting "autonomy."

Discussions about student choice often focus on *teachers* doing the thinking about what the choices can be and then offering students alternatives to pick. Student choice might also involve situations where there are multiple correct answers from which students can choose, but there is really a primary answer the teacher wants to lead them to (see "Inductive Learning" later in this chapter). These kinds of choice

 DOI: 10.4324/9781315208824-2

strategies can be effective in promoting autonomy, but there is also another way to support student autonomy—by encouraging student "voice."

Student voice is different from teachers giving "options." And it's *not* "empowerment"—a word disliked by most community organizers. It's not possible to empower—give power—to anyone, just as it's not possible to motivate anyone—at least if you want it to have any "staying" power. Instead, just as we can create the conditions where students can motivate themselves, we can create the conditions that support students *taking* power and using it.

In some cases, this could mean that instead of students reacting to teacher choices, they can take a proactive role in determining what those choices are to begin with. Other times, they could—with appropriate development and support—be in situations where they are making decisions using their own judgment independent of teacher-selected choices. Or, there might be circumstances where a teacher has broad goals for a lesson, but not necessarily a single "correct" answer in mind. Finally, "voice" can also mean actively soliciting student input on decisions affecting the class and acting on those recommendations (or, at least, many of them). These kinds of democratic classroom practices, in addition to supporting autonomy, have been directly related to increased academic achievement (Kahne et al., 2022).

Some researchers approach the ideas of student choice and voice through a slightly different lens, though ultimately agree with similar distinctions using different terminology. They divide student choice into three categories—organizational, procedural, and cognitive (Stefanou et al., 2004). An example of organizational choice might be having students help determine the due date for an assignment or participating in determining seating arrangements. A procedural choice could be having them decide what kind of media they would use to present an assignment or being able to select from a list of homework assignments. To explain cognitive choice, these researchers use a definition that is in some ways similar to how student "voice" was previously defined and suggest that its use tends to lead to more long-lasting feelings of autonomy. "Choice" and "voice" might both be described as supporting student "agency," where students feel they have power to act and help shape what is happening to them. It might be helpful to consider what the Latin roots of the word "agency" mean: "a mode of exerting power or producing effect," and "to set in motion, drive forward" (Online Etymology Dictionary, 2017).

Sometimes, in this book and in actual practice, the lines between "choice" and "voice" might be a bit fuzzy—and that's okay. Whatever you call it, any kind of promotion of student autonomy is recognition that power is not a finite "pie" that means my portion shrinks if you get some of it. Rather, the more power is shared—in the classroom or in society as a whole—the bigger the pie gets by creating more opportunities and possibilities for everyone.

What Are Ways Teachers Can Support Student Autonomy through Student Choice and Voice?

Ways to Promote Student Choice

Options not listed in any order of preference or effectiveness.

1. Letting Students Choose Who They Want to Work with in Small Group Learning

Research demonstrates the academic value of small group learning (Barron & Darling-Hammond, 2008).

There will be more discussion of its contribution towards intrinsic motivation in Chapter 4, but the focus here is on group composition. The tension is maximizing the "Relatedness" value of being able to work with who you want and minimizing cliquishness and some students feeling "left out."

I handle this challenge in a number of ways. At the beginning of the year, I explain to the class that as long as students take their work seriously and do good quality work, they will be able to freely choose whoever they want to work with for higher-stakes, multi-day group projects.

I go on to say, though, that we won't be doing any of those kinds of projects for the first several weeks. Instead, during this time, we'll do shorter group activities, ranging from two-minutes to most of a single period, where I will either be choosing partners or groups, or providing guidelines for who they can choose (no one can be wearing the same color socks, not everyone from the same culture, someone whom you don't know very well, etc.). These groupings will give everyone a chance to get to know each other, become more familiar with how they all work and often create opportunities for simple student choice. I also say we'll continue to do this kind of process for simple group activities throughout the year.

I then talk about how researchers have found that working with people who are different from ourselves—background, gender, ethnicity, etc.— can result in more creative and higher-quality work (Phillips, 2014) and sometimes I have students read an article summarizing those findings (searching "diverse small groups have better results" online will bring up many articles). I ask students to consider those studies when they choose their groups, and remind them of this research periodically during the year.

I also tell a joke that so many of us know, and have experienced, about the person who asks that members of their small group carry his casket when he has to be buried so that they could let him down one final time.

I share that between their experiences of working with classmates on short projects, and keeping in mind the research about diversity and the lesson taught by the joke, they will then have the knowledge they need to determine who are good matches when it is time to work together on longer-term projects.

When it is time for students to choose those groups, though, I also always give them the option to have me place them in a group—there might be some who are shy about making a choice. In those cases, I quickly have private conversations with one or two already-formed groups who almost always quickly agree to welcome the newcomer. Sometimes, I also give students an option to do a project on their own after explaining the importance of not going "solo" all the time because of the importance of developing cooperative skills that reflect what they will need to be doing in college and in future workplaces.

As you can see, creating the conditions for autonomy is not just a matter of telling students they can choose. It's a scaffolded and strategic process that helps students be autonomous *and* be successful. Students will not develop intrinsic motivation by having bad experiences and failing.

EDTECH TOOLBOX

Learn more about student small group logistics at "The Best Posts on the Basics of Small Groups in

the Classroom" (https://larryferlazzo.edublogs.
org/2011/09/18/my-best-posts-on-the-basics-
of-small-groups-in-the-classroom/).

2. Letting Students Choose Where They Sit

On the first day of school, I ask students to sit in desks in the order they enter the room, and fill up the desks one-by-one beginning with the seats in front. I explain that after I have memorized all their names in a week-or-two, students will complete a simple form expressing their seating preferences, and I'll use the results to create a new seating chart.

The form looks something like the one in Figure 2.1.

What Is "Autonomy" and Why Is it Important?

Seating Survey

Your Name _____

Do you want to stay where you are seated now?
Yes_____ No _____

If your answer is "No," what section of the room
would you like to sit in: Front _____ Back _____

If your answer is "No," please list names of
classmates—if any—you would like to sit
near you:

Is there anything else you would like me to know
that would help me create a new seating chart?

Figure 2.1   Seating survey for students.

When I distribute the survey, I emphasize that I can't guarantee that everyone will get the seat they want, but that I will try my best to accommodate their requests. I also explain that if they get a new seat, they can arrange to speak with me privately if they have concerns about it.

Some years, I distribute the seating survey just once, while other times two or three times, usually based on student request.

As all teachers know, during the school year it is possible that it may be best for some students to change seats because of discipline or concentration issues. When that is the case, I first have a private conversation with the student about that possibility and what he/she would need to do to stay in their present one. If nothing changes, I *always* provide them with at least two options for their new desk. If there are not enough empty seats available, I talk with two other students and ask them if they would be open to moving as a favor, but making it clear it is not required. If one is not open to moving, I talk to another.

EDTECH TOOLBOX

For additional ideas on student seating, explore "The Best Resources on Classroom Seating Strategies" (https://larryferlazzo.edublogs.org/2017/03/02/the-best-resources-on-classroom-seating-strategies/).

3. Using "Choice Boards"

Choice Boards are visual displays that show multiple alternatives of assignments or assessments. Students typically need to choose one (or possibly more for "extra credit"). Researchers have found them a particularly effective tool for differentiating instruction (Danley & Williams, 2020). An example from teacher Mary McNeal's English class can be found in Figure 2.2.

These alternatives obviously don't have to be displayed in a graphic organizer form. Instead, they can be shown as a list. For example, a teacher could just offer a simple list of writing prompts where students have to choose one; math problems or science questions where they have to choose two-or-three of them; or a list of alternative ways to make a presentation (slideshow, poster, skit, video, etc.).

Searching online for "choice boards" or for specific subject ones (for example, "science choice boards") will yield countless examples. Many digital versions are also available. See the EdTech Support Box for more resources.

What Is "Autonomy" and Why Is it Important?

SUPPORT MATERIAL

Book Project Choice Board		
Directions: Pick 1 activity to complete a book project.		
Crossword Puzzle	**Billboard**	**Diary Entries**
Describe at least twenty words in your book by creating a crossword puzzle and an answer key. You have to use the definition of your words as the clues. They must be vocabulary words that you have learned from reading this book.	Design a billboard based on information from the novel. It must have a theme from the story and advertise one character. Make sure that you create a colorful display of information that shows a complete understanding of the entire book you have read. You can include pictures, words, or anything else that will get your point across.	Pretend that you are the main character of the story. Write 10 diary entries that the character could have written. Seven of the entries should include information from the text that was read during the novel. Three of the entries should be written after the book has been read. (What do you think happened next for the character?) The journal entries should include the innermost thoughts of the character. Remember that you are writing the entries from his/her point of view.

Figure 2.2 Book project choice board created by Mary McNeal. Reprinted with permission.

What Is "Autonomy" and Why Is it Important?

Newspaper
Extra! Extra! Read all about it! What would the newspaper look like from the town the story takes place in? Here is your chance to show the rest of us. Create a newspaper. You should include a cover page, at least 2 articles based on events that have occurred in the novel, the weather of the town where the story takes place, or anything else that you feel is important.

Timeline
A novel is full of important events. Plot out at least 20 important events from the novel. Be as accurate as you can. Include a brief description and illustration about each event.

Travel Brochure
Make a travel brochure inviting tourists to visit the setting of the book. Include benefits of the setting as a vacation spot. For example, what activities does this spot offer, what historical landmarks can tourists see, and don't forget to include pictures.

Figure 2.2 Continued

SUPPORT MATERIAL

Alternate Ending	Red Carpet	ABC Book
Rewrite the ending of your book; write in the style of your author. DO NOT explain how the ending should be changed. Formulate it as if you were writing the story. This must be at least 2 typed pages. Use 12 point Times New Roman font.	The book has been turned into a movie. Who would play your favorite characters in the movie version? Pretend that you are going to be interviewing the cast along with the original characters from the book on the red carpet. What have the characters been up to since the end of the book? What do the actors think of the roles they are portraying? Write a newspaper article that includes this information. You must also design the movie poster that you saw at the event.	Create a children's ABC book. Include information from the novel for each letter of the alphabet. This can include characters, events, objects, etc. Make sure that you include the word, an illustration, and a description for each letter.

Figure 2.2 Continued

EDTECH TOOLBOX

In addition to finding tons of Choice Boards by searching online, you can find many examples of digital and graphic organizer versions for multiple subjects at "The Best Posts & Articles About Providing Students with Choices" (https://larryferlazzo.edublogs.org/2010/12/21/the-best-posts-articles-about-providing-students-with-choices/).

4. Providing Time for Independent Practice

The research-supported literacy practice of providing time for students to read books of their choosing (McQuillan, 2017) goes by a number of different names—Practice Reading, Silent Sustained Reading and Free Voluntary Reading are three of them. Students can choose physical books from a school or classroom library or read from one of many online reading sites (see the EdTech Support Box below for resources). This kind of reading can be an excellent way to begin class each day.

Another option is to have students use that time for other types of independent practice. For example, many websites provide a wide variety of student choice on their platforms, while others may use Artificial Intelligence for an adaptive learning system that guides students based on their responses to questions. To maintain the power of student choice, if one teacher-selected practice site is more guided, it would be important to have at least one other site alternative that is either also guided or that provides more choices. There are free or low-cost adaptive learning platforms for writing, grammar, and math. In addition, there are many sites that provide high-quality learning games in just about any content area. Finally, other sites provide countless articles on multiple topics provided at various reading levels—all ones that students can choose. For accountability purposes, most, if not all, require a Google log-in so that teachers can review student progress and use this information as an opportunity for formative assessment.

> **EDTECH TOOLBOX**
>
> Find links to many online tools that students can use to practice in any subject area at "The Best Sites Students Can Use for Independent Practice" (https://larryferlazzo.edublogs.org/2022/07/19/the-best-sites-students-can-use-for-independent-practice/).

5. Project or Problem-Based Learning

Two popular—and similar—group learning activities that provide opportunities for student choice are Project-Based Learning and Problem-Based Learning. Researchers have found that both are effective teaching and learning strategies (Terada, 2021; Yew & Goh, 2016).

Simply defined, Project-Based Learning usually means a small group works on a task that answers a common "driving question" (for example, "What are the qualities of an effective leader and how has someone we studied demonstrated them?") leading to a report or presentation (often students can choose what form the presentation takes—video, slideshow, poster, skit, etc.)—sometimes, though not always, to an "authentic audience" that is different from the class. Problem-Based Learning is similar, only that its task is generally a real-world problem that students must solve (such as "How can neighborhood residents be encouraged to complete U.S. Census forms?" or "How can our school make sure that students of color don't receive more office referrals than white students?"). An assignment using either activity can take anywhere from a day or two to several weeks to complete.

In both cases, teachers typically provide a question/task, planning forms, a timeline and guidelines for the activity. Sometimes students can be provided with a broad topic (for example, "local history" for Project-Based Learning or "ways to improve our school" for Problem-Based Learning) and then they can be asked to identify a narrower question or focus for their academic task.

See the EdTech Support Box for resources on how to get started with each type of these cooperative learning activities.

EDTECH TOOLBOX

Go to "The Best Resources for Learning How to Use Project-Based Learning & Problem-Based Learning in Your Classroom" (https://larryfer lazzo.edublogs.org/2022/07/19/the-best-resources-for-learning-how-use-project-based-learning-problem-based-learning-in-your-classroom/) for practical tools for using Project-Based Learning and Problem-Based Learning in your classroom.

6. "Genius Hour"

"Genius Hour" is the name given to school projects that reflect practices initiated by private companies that give time to their employees to work on projects of their choice. Google's practice of giving many of its employees 20% of their time to devote to their own ideas is probably the most well-known version of this activity in the private sector.

In the classroom, a "Genius Hour" is basically an activity where students—who can choose to work individually or in a group—decide on a topic they want to learn about, do research, and share their results (sometimes as a slideshow presentation or as a TED-like talk). Typically, students are given a fairly broad latitude to determine their topic (which, of course, must be approved by the teacher), and then follow a set sequence of tasks leading to their presentation.

I have also done versions of a Genius Hour that are a little more prescriptive and which have also gone well. For example, in my World History class, students near the end of the school year had to choose a person or event they wanted to learn more about. Other times, students had to instruct the class, or in small groups, about their topic using specific teaching strategies we used during the year that promoted higher-order thinking skills (such as "inductive" lessons—explained more later in this chapter), or "clozes," also known as "gap-fills".

There is limited research on the academic effectiveness of Genius Hour in schools, though many of Google's most successful products have come out of employee's use of their twenty percent time (Murphy, 2020). Nevertheless, in addition to encouraging student choice, a Genius Hour can create many opportunities for standards-based work, including in research, writing, presenting, and speaking.

A short amount of time could be devoted to a Genius Hour project each day for several weeks, or it could be the main focus of student work for several days. I've found that an activity like this works especially well leading up to a holiday break or immediately prior to the end of the school year.

Additional related ideas and resources on students teaching their classmates can be found in Chapter 3.

> ## EDTECH TOOLBOX
>
> Practical tools for organizing a Genius Hour (or a version of it) in your classroom can be found at "The Best Resources For Applying "Fed Ex Days" (Also Known As "Genius Hours") To Schools" (https://larryferlazzo.edublogs.org/2012/05/28/the-best-resources-for-applying-fed-ex-days-to-schools/) and at "The Best Posts On Helping Students Teach Their Classmates—Help Me Find More" (https://larryferlazzo.edublogs.org/2012/04/22/the-best-posts-on-helping-students-teach-their-classmates-help-me-find-more/).

7. Inductive Learning

Teaching inductively means students are given a variety of carefully selected examples and, then, on their own or in a group, need to determine the concept or category that those examples demonstrate. *Inductive* teaching contrasts with *deductive* teaching, which is when the teacher explicitly explains the concept or category and then provides examples that reinforce them. Substantial research has found the inductive teaching method particularly effective for student learning (Obeidat & Alomari, 2020; Prince & Felder, 2006).

In inductive teaching and learning, therefore, students are autonomously *constructing* their knowledge as opposed to *receiving* it. They are like detectives looking for patterns.

Two ways that I apply this teaching are through the use of inductive data sets and concept attainment.

Inductive data sets are lists of exemplars that students have to place into categories that share common characteristics. These exemplars could be as short as a word or a sentence, or as long as a paragraph. A data set could include items demonstrating the different elements of an essay (Hook, Thesis Statement, Topic Sentence, Claim, Evidence, Conclusion) or, in Social Studies, the different categories involved in describing a country (Geography, Demographics, Economy, Political System, Culture). Similar data sets, which could also be physical items or images, can be used in all subject areas. Categories could be provided to students beforehand or they could be asked to formulate their own (especially after they gain experience with this kind of activity).

Students then have to place the items into categories of their choice, which often will fit into the ones expected by the teacher. The key is that students must provide evidence for their choices and any answer backed-up by sufficient evidence is correct. The "extension" activity for these inductive data sets is where the power of choice really comes into play for students—once the data set items are sorted into categories, students are then challenged to identify additional items on their own that fit into each of them.

A simple data set about San Francisco that I use in my English Language Learner class can be found in Figure 2.3. This example includes my giving the categories ahead of time, though could easily be used with student-created groupings.

What Is "Autonomy" and Why Is it Important?

	SAN FRANCISCO DATA SET
	History; Weather; Interesting Places to See
1.	In 1775, Juan Manuel de Ayala was the first person from Europe to visit the area that became San Francisco.
2.	It does not snow in San Francisco.
3.	San Francisco grew from 500 people to 25,000 people in 1849 after gold was discovered in California.
4.	Sixty-seven people died in San Francisco after an earthquake in 1989.
5.	There was a prison on Alcatraz Island in the San Francisco Bay.
6.	San Francisco is famous for its cable cars. Cable cars are like little buses.
7.	At least fifteen thousand Chinese-Americans live in Chinatown in San Francisco.
8.	Sea lions live on Fisherman's Wharf.
9.	The water in San Francisco Bay is very cold.
10.	The Golden Gate Bridge goes over San Francisco Bay.
11.	Coit Tower was built to honor firefighters.
12.	There is fog in San Francisco on many days.
13.	Half of San Francisco was destroyed by an earthquake and fire in 1906.
14.	Members of the Ohlone or Costanoan Native American tribes were the first people to live in the San Francisco area before the Spanish came.
15.	It usually does not get too hot in San Francisco during the summer.
16.	Golden Gate Park is a very big park in San Francisco.

Figure 2.3 Concept Obtainment Example. A version of this data set originally appeared in *Helping Students Motivate Themselves*. Reproduced with permission. Copyright 2011. Routledge/Taylor & Francis, Inc. New York, NY. All rights reserved. Routledge.com/k-12.

Concept Attainment is the other inductive strategy I often use in class. In Concept Attainment, correct and incorrect exemplars of the concept being taught (what makes a good "claim," the correct use of the verb "have") are displayed. Students have to then work on their own or in groups to explain the reason or reasons why some are under "yes" and others under "no." Once they understand the "rule" or "rules," they then have to extend and demonstrate their understanding by developing their own "yes" and "no" exemplars. As with the data set strategy, student choice particularly is present in the extension activity.

A simple concept attainment model I use with my ELL class can be found in Figure 2.4. It's designed to teach "is" and "are." Two other elements of the Concept Attainment strategy to keep in mind— I generally unveil the different yes and no examples one at a time and give students time in between to figure out the answer (though sharing them all at once can work, too) and, if I use it to teach writing, I will often use student writing examples (with their permission).

What Is "Autonomy" and Why Is it Important?

Yes	No
Jose is a boy.	
	Asma are a girl.
The book is blue.	
	The car are red.
Juan and Carol are students.	
	Ma and Der is sisters.
Ari, Pachoua, and Rafael are on the soccer team.	
	Patty, Bob, and Chia is excellent students.

Figure 2.4 Concept attainment example.

Though the two Inductive Teaching Figures used here are designed for English Language Learners, I have used much more complex texts for ones used in my International Baccalaureate classes and for professional development sessions with teachers. Many other examples can be found at the resource in the EdTech Support Box and in my other books.

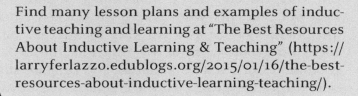

EDTECH TOOLBOX

Find many lesson plans and examples of inductive teaching and learning at "The Best Resources About Inductive Learning & Teaching" (https://larryferlazzo.edublogs.org/2015/01/16/the-best-resources-about-inductive-learning-teaching/).

Ways to Promote Student Voice (options not listed in any order of preference or effectiveness)

8. Creating a Class "Mission" Statement

I'm not a big fan of spending time at the beginning of a school year co-creating classroom "rules" with students. I always just announce that the key rule is "Be respectful, including not touching other people's stuff." I think that one covers the most important issues.

Instead, I think it's far more important and productive to spend time co-creating a broader sense of "mission."

Not only will students' sense of autonomy be strengthened by the initial process of making choices for a mission statement, but having to connect it to everyday occurrences throughout the year will be another avenue for reinforcement of that autonomy.

I use a fairly simple one class period process near the beginning of the year where students decide if they want to be part of a "classroom of students" or a "community of learners." A detailed lesson plan for it can be found in one of my previous books (Ferlazzo, 2013a, p. 52). However, teacher Kristin Elam wrote an excellent summary of how she applied the lesson (Ferlazzo, 2013b). Here is Kristin's summary:

> This year we have eliminated tracking in our 9th grade English classes and as such we have sought out ways to help build community and reconnect our students who have been tracked since 4th grade. We are also working to increase our focus on group work as we integrate the CCSS [Common Core State Standards] and prepare students from the group work element of the SBAC [state-required standardized tests].
>
> Today in class we started with a quick intro to the CCSS and the increase in group work and critical thinking that will go along with CCSS, which easily led us to the "Community of Learners." First, the students did a think/write—pair—share for each of the four categories. We then had a general discussion on the differences between a town and a community where we identified what makes a community different (i.e. knowing each other well and supporting each other). Next I projected a quote often attributed to W. B. Yeats: "Education is not the filling of a pail but the lighting of a fire" (note that my EL population didn't know what a "pail" was!), and had them think-pair-share what they thought the quote means. Finally they decided which part of the quote would go into which column of our chart.
>
> We then further discussed the categories of a "classroom of students" vs a "community of learners", clarifying the difference between the two.

Once they seemed to have a clear understanding, I had them share ideas with their partner for each of the next three rows and then we combined their ideas into our class chart. Finally, they wrote a paragraph reflection on which of the two classrooms they would prefer and why. I collected the paragraphs as an initial writing sample for me to keep on file.

After completing our lesson and deciding that we would like to try to be a community of learners as much as possible, we moved into our first big CCSS lesson on "close reading" adapted from Odell Education in NY. The first lesson in the "Brain Gain" unit focuses on using guiding questions to analyze two photographs, which happen to be of a classroom 60 years ago and a classroom today. Several students made a connection that I had not previously made that one classroom looked like a classroom of students and one looked like a community of learners! It was great to hear them carrying over the earlier lesson to a completely different context and medium. I think the lesson was a great introduction to how I want my classroom to run without me just having stood up there and told them what my rules and expectations are for the year.

Figure 2.5 is reprinted from the lesson plan in my book. The outline should be blank as students offer their own ideas—the content in the example is there to give teachers some ideas of what might be included.

What Is "Autonomy" and Why Is it Important?

	Classroom of Students	Community of Learners
Role of teacher	Teaches, lectures, "fills pail," does most of the talking, delivers all information to students	Doesn't know all the answers, helps students to teach themselves and other students, learns from students, "lights the fire"
Role of students	Sit quietly and listen, think the teacher is always right	Talk and learn from one another, help the teacher become better by giving constructive feedback, ask questions, are cocreators of their learning environment
What motivates students	Grades, points, extra credit, fear of punishment	"The reward of a thing well done is to have done it," wanting to learn
What happens when a student makes a mistake or does something well?	Ridicule, jealousy, rudeness, "You're dumb!" "Oooh, Johnny's a brain!"	"People are celebrated for taking risks, for learning from mistakes, and for doing exceptionally good work. Students are courteous and want their classmates to be

Figure 2.5 Compare and contrast chart. Reproduced with permission from Ferlazzo, *Self-Driven Learning: Teaching Strategies for Student Motivation.* Copyright 2013: Routledge/Taylor & Francis, Inc. New York, NY. All rights reserved. Routledge.com/k-12

9. Setting Up Student Leadership Teams

During the first two months of the school year, I try to keep an eye out for students who have potential leadership skills. In other words, who are the students who seem to have the respect of at least some of their classmates and who seem to be good "thinkers"? This group often includes both those with higher *and* those with lower grades. It also has as members students whom I regularly interact with because of their behavior and those who never need my intervention.

I then privately approach each and say they seem to have leadership skills and be good thinkers, being sure to share specific examples. I tell them that I organize "Leadership Teams" in each of my classes, composed of students who have those qualities. Members of the team take responsibility to help lead small groups in class, welcome new students, model participation in class discussions, and provide feedback to me about how to improve the class. They also eventually need to help identify and mentor new members for the Team, and complete a simple weekly Google Form to help them reflect on how they are doing as class leaders. The Team meets with me every other week for a few minutes while the rest of the class is doing an activity, like practice reading or working on a project.

I don't believe anyone has ever refused my invitation, and many have seemed surprised and/or honored by receiving one.

After I have spoken with each person individually, I introduce the Leadership Team to the class and, at the same time, invite anyone else who might be interested in participating to talk with me privately.

In meetings, I remind Team members that they always have a responsibility to be leaders in any small group they are part of, including making sure that everyone feels heard and stays on task, and need to be prepared to give feedback on what they feel is going well in class and how they think it can be improved. I often include very short "trainings" on leadership development during the Team meetings.

You can see the reflection questions Team members need to answer each week in Figure 2.6. Most of the questions have "linear scale" responses where they click any number ranging from one-to-five (one meaning "Not so great" while five meaning "great"), while others require short written answers.

	Reflection Questions for Class Leadership Team Members
1.	How would you rate how you've done helping lead small groups this past week?
2.	How would you rate how you did in small groups to get everyone participating?
3.	How would you rate how you did in modeling being kind, welcoming, and friendly to others in our class this past week? Did you try to invite new people who might not know people into your small groups?
4.	How would you rate yourself in contributing to whole class discussions by sharing your thoughts or asking questions?
5.	How would you rate yourself this past week in acting as a co-teacher when we're in the whole class by helping to answer student questions, respectfully pointing out to Mr. Ferlazzo when he's making a mistake, or clarifying any confusion?
6.	We have students in our class who are still learning English. How would you rate yourself as trying to be welcoming and helpful to those particular students?
7.	Is there anyone else in this class you think you could encourage and mentor to eventually also join the leadership team? If so, who do you think it could be?
8.	What are your suggestions about what Mr. Ferlazzo can do to make the class better for everyone?
9.	How would you like to improve as a leader over the next week? What do you want to work on?

SUPPORT MATERIAL

Figure 2.6   Reflection questions for class leadership team members (Ferlazzo & Hull-Sypnieski, 2022, p. 275).

Class Leadership Teams have had a huge positive impact on my classes over the years. An added benefit for students is that many have loved being able to list their participation on college applications!

EDTECH TOOLBOX

Tools and ideas I've found helpful in developing the short trainings on leadership development I use for the Class Leadership Team meetings can be found at "A Beginning List of the Best Resources on Learning about Leadership" (https://larryferl azzo.edublogs.org/2021/06/17/a-beginning-list-of-the-best-resources-on-learning-about-leader ship-share-your-own/).

10. Anonymous Class and Teacher Evaluations

Extensive research has found that teachers soliciting student feedback on classes and their teaching can be powerful learning opportunities (Scott, 2021). I typically have students complete anonymous evaluations at least twice each year and often several times—doing it only at the end of the year means there is no time to make adjustments based on student feedback.

Another reason for doing these evaluations during the year is that teachers can publicly acknowledge the results, along with telling students what they will do differently or the same based on them. The only thing worse than not doing an evaluation—or any kind of survey at all—is doing them and then ignoring the results. In that case, not only will student "voice," sense of autonomy, and intrinsic motivation not be encouraged, but the opposite will occur.

Remember what Chapter 1 said about the importance of "baseline rewards"—if students feel like teachers are only going through the motions of listening to their opinion and not valuing it, "amotivation" (the absence of motivation) can be the result.

That doesn't mean we *have* to change anything based on evaluation results. But teachers may learn that students need to get better explanations from us about what we are doing and why we are doing it.

It's not absolutely necessary, but I always announce to students ahead of time that I will share the results of the evaluations publicly in my blog and with school administrators. I believe that knowledge may prompt them to take the job of completing the evaluation more seriously than they might otherwise. Of course, if you implement that kind of strategy, you never know who will read it— The Washington Post once picked up on my blog post about the evaluation results from one class and reprinted them with the headline *NEWS BREAK (not breaking news): Teacher asks students to grade him. One wrote: "I give Mr. Ferlazzo an A at being annoying."* (Strauss, 2019).

I have learned *so much* over the years from these evaluations, and become a much better teacher because of them.

These kinds of evaluations can take many different forms. Figure 2.7 is a simple Google Form I have used that has most questions answered in a one-to-five linear scale, along with space for a few short narrative responses.

Anonymous Class Evaluation	
1.	How did you generally feel about this class?
2.	How interesting was the content of this class?
3.	How organized was the Google Classroom for this class?
4.	How fair was grading for this class?
5.	How did you feel about the quantity of work that was required for this class?
6.	How did you feel about Mr. Ferlazzo's teaching ability?
7.	How did you feel that Mr. Ferlazzo cared about you as an individual person, as opposed to "just another student in class"?
8.	What was the most interesting thing you learned in this class?
9.	What was the best thing about this class?
10.	What was the worst thing about this class and how do you think it could be improved?

Figure 2.7 Anonymous class evaluation (Ferlazzo & Hull-Sypnieski, 2022, p. 482).

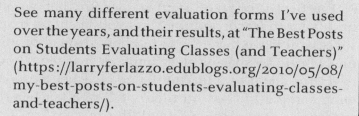

EDTECH TOOLBOX

See many different evaluation forms I've used over the years, and their results, at "The Best Posts on Students Evaluating Classes (and Teachers)" (https://larryferlazzo.edublogs.org/2010/05/08/my-best-posts-on-students-evaluating-classes-and-teachers/).

11. Giving Advice to Others

Studies indicate that putting students in positions where they have to give advice can help the person receiving the advice, enhance autonomy of the student giving the advice and also increase the advisor's academic performance (Sparks, 2022; Thibodeaux, 2022).

Once a week, my Junior students (after receiving training) function as mentors and take ninth-graders out for a ten-minute "walk-and-talk." In addition to checking-in with how their mentees are generally doing, they get a "focus" question each time ("What are you most worried about today?" or "What do you want people to say about you twenty years from now?"). Our school has been able to replicate studies that show students who volunteered to be mentors increased their grades more than those who did not (Ferlazzo, 2019).

Another way I've promoted the idea of "advice-giving" was originally prompted by an article I read in The Harvard Business Review which suggested that prior to doing just about any task it was worthwhile asking yourself *"Who else (apart from myself) is going to benefit from what I am doing?"* (Keller & Webb, 2017).

What Is "Autonomy" and Why Is it Important?

In some years, and in some classes, I use that question to begin an initiative I call "Everyone Is A Teacher" (Ferlazzo, 2017). I explain that we all have a lot to learn, and the class will likely be more successful if we have thirty teachers instead of just one. I begin by sharing an example or two about how everyone could be a teacher ("I'm a teacher by modeling coming to class on time" or "I'm a teacher by modeling not texting my friends during class" or "I'm a teacher when I help a student who doesn't understand something"), and then invite students to create individual "I'm A Teacher When I . . ." posters. We may spend time brainstorming different ideas prior to making posters. We hang them on the wall, and I periodically ask students to reflect on what they've done recently "to be a teacher."

EDTECH TOOLBOX

More details on how our school organizes and runs our mentor program, as well as information on other similar efforts, can be found at "The Best Resources on the Value & Practice of Having Older Students Mentoring Younger Ones" (https://larryferlazzo.edublogs.org/2013/02/03/the-best-resources-on-the-value-practice-of-having-older-students-mentoring-younger-ones/).

12. Students Making their Own Goals

Research finds that goal-setting, and subsequently achieving them, can encourage motivation through the development of autonomy and competence (Fletcher-Wood, 2019).

I have tried *many* different strategies to facilitate students setting goals and monitoring their own progress. Resources in The EdTech Support Box document all of them. Many have had limited or zero success.

Here are three goal-setting strategies that I use now which *appear* to have had some positive impact on student motivation and achievement.

"Big-To-Little"

1. First, students reflect and share about times in the past they have set a goal and achieved it, along with what helped make them successful. Students then determine two longer-term "big" goals: One is the kind of career they want to pursue (they can share multiple ones) and the other is what they want other people to say about their lives forty years in the future ("She was a good doctor who helped a lot of sick people get better" or "He brought joy to many people through the video games he designed"). This "far future" goal comes from author Daniel Pink's "One Sentence Project." Though it's obviously not a complicated question, you can see the EdTech Support Box for supporting materials, including videos, that can help make student development of these "one sentences" a more engaging process. These are then shared publicly, often in posters that are hung on the classroom walls and discussed verbally with classmates. Research shows that sharing goals publicly, particularly with those who you respect, increases the chances of success (Dean, 2006).

2. Students then identify at least three things they can do *now* to help them achieve those two "bigger" goals—at least two of which need to be related to school. These are also shared publicly.

3. After some time has passed, I then meet with each student individually and share a blank number line from zero to one-hundred. We go over each of the three actions they identified, and they mark on the number line where they think they are in terms of effort and success in making those happen. I then ask them if they are satisfied with that effort and success or if they would like it to be higher on the number line.

4. If they say they are happy with their degree of effort and success, I tell them "Great!" and ask for suggestions on what I can do to support them. If they indicate they would like to be at a higher level, I ask them "What would it take to get there?" and we discuss additional actions they can take, and ways I can support them.

5. I periodically ask students to reflect—in writing and verbally—how they feel they are progressing on their goals, which is sometimes shared publicly. I also regularly talk with students individually, and refer back to their self-identified goals. In addition, I remind students that it's okay to adjust their goals—priorities change.

This autonomous process has seemed to be fairly successful as a self-motivating strategy. It has also served as an extraordinarily effective classroom management tool—when a student is being off-task, I can point to their long-term goals hanging on the wall and ask "Is what you are doing now going to help you get there?" I feel much better about saying that instead of, "Paul, please get back to work." In addition, research suggests that asking this kind of goal-related question is actually more effective at getting people to refocus than an admonition (Ferlazzo, 2012).

Daily Goal

Another goal-setting strategy that I have sometimes used as an entire class and other times just with individual students is to ask them at the beginning of a class to identify either a Social Emotional Learning goal they have for that day or a more academically oriented one. For SEL, I offer ideas like "I want to be more focused in class"; "I want to help another student"; "I want to compliment someone," or "I want to ask someone how they are doing." I offer the academic goal option if they already know what we are going to do that day, so they might be able to say "I want to complete our presentation" or "I want to write at least three-hundred words in my essay." Students share their goal verbally with a partner and, then, at the end of class, I generally have people anonymously write either "yes" or "no" on a piece of paper that I collect indicating if they achieved their goal or not as well as giving them the option to share their experience with a new partner. I use this process once-or-twice a month.

Weekly Goal

In Chapter 4, I share a weekly Google Form that students complete. Two of the questions are "What is one goal you want to achieve this week?" and "Did you achieve your goal last week?" It's simple, but students have commented positively on the questions.

EDTECH TOOLBOX

For additional research on goal-setting, and to see documentation of twenty years of different classroom attempts at implementing student goal-setting activities, visit "The Best Posts on Students Setting Goals" (https://larryferlazzo. edublogs.org/2010/05/18/my-best-posts-on-students-setting-goals/). Resources to help students create "one sentences" can be found at "The Best Resources for Doing a 'One-Sentence Project'" (https://larryferlazzo.edublogs.org/2013/03/13/ the-best-resources-for-doing-a-one-sentence-project/).

13. Self-Behavior Management

"Classroom Management," as most teachers know, is a term used to describe ways to ensure that students behave at school in a way that facilitates learning. Unfortunately, I sometimes see it viewed as an end in itself, instead of it just being one element that's needed along the way towards the goal of students gaining knowledge. As the Civil Rights Movement anthem suggests, we teachers are better served if we "keep our eyes on the prize" (Trescott, 2011) and recognize that orderliness is a necessity in creating a classroom of learners, but rigidity is not.

Researchers have found that often self-control is not necessarily just a matter of demonstrating will-power. Instead, it can be exhibited when people are in a position of wanting and liking to do the things that others might resist (Resnick, 2020). Creating the conditions that support intrinsic motivation— autonomy, competence, relatedness and relevance— are good starts towards making learning in class more of something that students *want* to do instead of forcing themselves to *persevere* through it (Shafer, 2018). Famed educator William Glasser believed that students have a basic need for power and to be listened to, and that 95 percent of classroom management issues occur as a result of students trying to fulfill this need (Jones, 2015). Further research has shown that the more power people feel they have, the more self-control they tend to exhibit so student "choice" should be a positive contributor to student self-behavior management.

As I have mentioned previously, though, I also "live in the world as it is." I place a major emphasis on supporting students to develop intrinsic motivation, but my wonderful students who I like and care deeply for are still sometimes off-task, disruptive, and annoying (to their classmates and to me). They are kids, after all (of course, those same descriptions could be applied to many adults, too).

All the listed strategies in this book can contribute towards helping students develop self-behavior management skills. Here is a process I use to specifically promote the development of those skills *and* student autonomy:

1. With little or no introduction, I show students a six-minute TED Talk about the famous Marshmallow Test (de Posada, 2009). In this experiment, pre-schoolers were given a marshmallow by a researcher and told that if they didn't eat it before the adult returned, they would then get two marshmallows. Scientists tracked the children through adulthood and found that those who resisted temptation tended to be more successful as they grew older than those who did not.

2. After showing the video, which is a fun way to introduce the topic to students, I explain that there are some recent questions about its validity, but many researchers have still found that

self-control can have a role in people's success (Schwartz, 2016; Toppo, 2018). I usually then go around and put some kind of treat on everyone's desk and explain that we will have our own version of The Marshmallow Test today—if it's still there by the end of the class, they'll get a second one. Doing this not only adds more fun to the experience, but it also serves as a positive reinforcement because students almost always are able to wait. I also point out that new versions of this experiment don't use marshmallows, and ask students what they think are used instead. They *always* accurately say cell phone notifications and texts (Herrera, 2018; Sparks, 2012).

3. I then explain that researchers use the term "self-deployed interventions" to describe actions that we can take to develop better self-control (Duckworth et al., 2018). These include:

- Making "if-then" plans for the future ("If I feel like I'm getting distracted, I'll ask the teacher if I can step outside for a minute-or-two").
- Modifying situations (such as keeping a cell-phone in your backpack during class so you don't see or hear it).
- Setting goals and remembering them (see the previous goal-setting activities).
- Thinking about potential obstacles to goals and, ahead of time, developing plans to overcome them ("One of my goals today is to get this essay done. I like to talk to my friend in the next desk, so if I find that's distracting I'll ask the teacher if I can move to the back for the day").
- Mindfulness (I sometimes do visualization exercises with students—see the EdTech Support Box).

4. Students then write about times they've successfully used these strategies in the past and share with partners. They then write in their notebooks or make posters identifying one or more self-control challenges they think they have (I always model my own first) and one or more "self-deployed interventions" they can apply when they come up. Students share what they wrote with classmates, I create opportunities during the year for them to reflect on how they are doing with them, and I also mention them when needed.

EDTECH TOOLBOX

Much more information can be found about self-control research, and my successes and failures in applying it to the classroom, at "The Best Posts about Helping Students Develop Their Capacity for Self-Control" (https://larryferlazzo. edublogs.org/2010/06/03/my-best-posts-about-helping-students-develop-their-capacity-for-self-control/). See "Best Posts on Helping Students 'Visualize Success'" (https://larryferlazzo.edublogs.org/2010/12/23/my-best-posts-on-helping-students-visualize-success/) for ideas on how to use visualization with students.

---

14. Self-Assessment

Researchers have identified student self-assessment as a contributor toward productive learning (Panadero et al., 2017). There are many ways to incorporate this practice in classrooms and the EdTech Support Box can share many of them.

Here, though, I would primarily like to talk about student self-assessment for quarter and semester grades. I always have students grade themselves— in both narrative and letter-grade form—and ninety percent of the time their self-assessments line-up with mine. When it doesn't, they can make an evidence-based case for their grade, and it sometimes has worked.

I always share the assessment "instrument" at the beginning of the year, so students know what I'm looking for. Figures 2.8 and 2.9 are two examples of assessment forms I've sometimes used and more can be found via the EdTech Support Box.

What Is "Autonomy" and Why Is it Important?

Self-Assessment Form
If I disagree with you, we will meet individually & you can make your case.
Name: **Period:**
Personal Grade Reflection—Answer and Give supporting examples (you may write on back)
Do you initiate working and learning most or all of the time in this class, or does Mr. Ferlazzo have to push you a lot?
Do you take risks and try challenging tasks in this class even if you make mistakes (and learn from them). Or do you "play it safe" most of the time?
Do you try to teach other students if you understand something more than they do? Do you just give them the answer, or do you help them learn? Or do you only focus on your own work and ignore students who need help?
When you don't feel like doing the assignment, most of the time do you do your best anyway, or do you try to put it off and/or not do your best or not do it at all?
Are you respectful of your classmates and Mr. Ferlazzo? In other words, do you listen when they are speaking, are you serious when you are presenting to the class and thoughtful when asking questions of presenters?
Think about the answers you made to the last four questions, and think about the quality of your school work this quarter—tests, classwork, computer assignments, etc. What grade do you think you deserve and why?

Figure 2.8   Self-assessment form.

What Is "Autonomy" and Why Is it Important?

Grade Reflection	
Name:	**Period:**
	Researchers have found that several qualities are important for a person to be a successful learner. Please answer each question. Then, take some time to reflect on all of your answers and give yourself the grade that you believe you have earned in this class. If the grade you decide is higher than I believe is appropriate, we will meet and you will have an opportunity to convince me that you are correct. In the seven years students have graded themselves, I have either agreed with their grade or believed they earned a higher one than they had thought ninety percent of the time. Five percent of the time where there has been the other kind of difference students have persuaded me to go along with their position.
	SELF-CONTROL: How do you act in class? Do you pay attention when your classmates and/or Mr. Ferlazzo is speaking or do you often talk with a neighbor or text during those times? Can you restrain yourself from eating at inappropriate times, or are you unable to stop yourself even when it distracts you and your classmates from a learning task?

Figure 2.9 Grade reflection.

SUPPORT MATERIAL

PERSEVERANCE: Do you do your best work most of the time? Do you give your best effort even when you are not that interested in the learning task? Or do you typically do the least amount you believe you can get away with?

CONSCIENTIOUSNESS: Do you do your homework and classwork on time? Do you keep track of your assignments? Is your class folder or binder organized and up-to-date?

CURIOSITY: Do you work to find something of interest in whatever we are studying, even though on the surface it might not "grab you." Do you think of thoughtful questions to ask your classmates during presentations, to write down when you are reading, or to ask Mr. Ferlazzo? Do you try to "stretch yourself"?

Figure 2.9 Continued

What Is "Autonomy" and Why Is it Important?

ETHICS: Have you generally acted ethically? In other words, have you done your own work and not copied from a classmate or plagiarized from a book or from the Internet when you could have done so and would likely not have been discovered?

GIVING: Adam Grant, an author and researcher, suggests that people are generally one of three types: givers, takers and matchers. Givers tend to help others without always expecting something in return; Takers ten to look out for themselves and take advantage of others; and matchers ten to only give when they can expect to get something back. Grant suggests that people who are Givers are the ones who are most successful in life. In this class, have you tended to be a giver, taker or matcher?

Figure 2.9 Continued

MASTERY: How well do you think you've learned the concepts we have explored in class? Have you "mastered" it? In other words, do you know enough of the key ideas to be able to explain it to others and to apply them to your own life?

FINAL GRADE: Reflect on your answers to all of the previous seven questions. What grade do you believe you have earned in this class? Feel free to provide any additional evidence to support your position that you have not described earlier.

Figure 2.9 Continued

EDTECH TOOLBOX

You can find many more ideas on implement student self-assessment at "The Best Resources on Grading Practices" (https://larryferlazzo.edublogs.org/2013/01/09/the-best-resources-on-grading-practices/) and at "The Best Resources on Student Self-Assessment" (https://larryferlazzo.edublogs.org/2018/07/24/the-best-resources-on-student-self-assessment/).

The fourteen strategies that have been described here are just a "drop in the bucket." As mentioned in Chapter 1, we all have opportunities each day to take small and simple actions to promote student autonomy, such as giving students the option of completing an assignment on paper or online, or, after they have become familiar with multiple reading strategies to use, instead of assigning a specific one, we can tell them to use whichever they feel would be most helpful to them.

The list may not be endless, but it sure is darn long . . .

What Questions Can Teachers Ask Themselves to Ensure Their Strategies to Promote Student Autonomy Are Also Culturally Responsive?

Can students see themselves in the materials I use while implementing these strategies (such as exemplars in data sets and books in my classroom libraries) and in any materials I might display on the classroom walls to support the lessons?

Am I looking for opportunities to emphasize student assets (such as asking them to share about their successes in demonstrating self-control in the past before approaching the challenges they may be experiencing now) instead of leading by looking at their so-called "deficits"?

Am I maximizing the chances for all students' voices to be heard in each activity (for example, encouraging as many students as possible to publicly share their goals), or am I rushing through it because of artificial time constraints?

Am I demonstrating explicit or implicit bias in any of my actions? For example, when I approach students for the Class Leadership Team, are its members diverse in gender, race and culture?

Am I differentiating instruction so that the learning activities are accessible to everyone, including English Language Learners and those students with learning differences. For example, when showing the Marshmallow Test video, am I showing it at a slower speed, using English subtitles or subtitles in the home language of Newcomer students? Am I providing sentence starters for those who need it when writing is required? Do I provide home language support when and if necessary?

When dividing into small group activities, am I working to make sure any English Language Learners have a "buddy" who might or might not share their home language, but who has voluntarily agreed to be particularly supportive of them? This accommodation is especially important for larger projects, such as Project or Problem Based Learning.

When I give examples for students when choosing topics to study during Project and Problem-Based Learning activities or during Genius Hours, do I make a point of including home culture, anti-racist, and community improvement topics, and do I support students if they identify ideas in those categories for their projects?

Am I looking for ways to develop home-school connections? For example, do I encourage students to see their families as resources for their Project & Problem-Based Learning, and for their Genius Hour activities, as well as considering them as possible audiences to view and hear the final projects? Do I maintain avenues to communicate with families about classroom activities, including using online tools that provide multilingual support?

Do I monitor if students are being respectful of each other's identities? For example, do I make sure that students' preferred pronouns are respected in class and that mentors are doing the same with their mentees?

EDTECH TOOLBOX

The questions at the end of this chapter and throughout the book are just a *few* introductory ways educators can integrate culturally responsiveness into their teaching. You can learn many more at "The Best Resources About 'Culturally Responsive Teaching' & 'Culturally Sustaining Pedagogy'—Please Share More!" (https://larryferlazzo.edublogs.org/2016/06/10/the-best-resources-about-culturally-responsive-teaching-culturally-sustaining-pedagogy-please-share-more/).

References

Barron, B., & Darling-Hammond, L. (2008, October 8). Powerful learning: Studies show deep understanding derives from collaborative methods. *Edutopia.* www.edutopia.org/inquiry-project-learning-research

Danley, A., & Williams, C. (2020). Choice in learning: Differentiating instruction in the college classroom. *InSight: A Journal of Scholarly Teaching, 15,* 83–104.

de Posada, J. (Director). (2009, May). Don't eat the marshmallow. www.ted.com/talks/joachim_de_posada_don_t_eat_the_marshmallow

Dean, J. (2006, June). The simplest strategy to boost motivation. *PsyBlog.* www.spring.org.uk/2022/06/boost-mot.php

Duckworth, A. L., Milkman, K. L., & Laibson, D. (2018). Beyond willpower: Strategies for reducing failures of self-control. *Psychological Science in the Public Interest, 19*(3), 102–129. https://doi.org/10.1177/1529100618821893

Ferlazzo, L. (2011). *Helping students motivate themselves: Practical answers to classroom challenges.* Eye on Education.

Ferlazzo, L. (2012, June 22). Being reminded of the consequences of losing self-control doesn't help; asking about goals does. *Larry Ferlazzo's Website of the Day.* https://larryferlazzo.edublogs.org/2012/06/22/being-reminded-of-the-consequences-of-losing-self-control-doesnt-help-asking-about-goals-does/)

Ferlazzo, L. (2013a). *Self-driven learning: Teaching strategies for student motivation.* Eye on Education.

Ferlazzo, L. (2013b, August 8). Do we want a "community of learners" or a "classroom of students"? *Larry Ferlazzo's Website of the Day.* https://larryferlazzo.edublogs.org/2013/08/08/do-we-want-a-community-of-learners-or-a-classroom-of-students/

Ferlazzo, L. (2017, March 23). "Everyone is a teacher" is a new engagement strategy I'm using & it seems to be working. *Larry Ferlazzo's Website of the Day.* https://larryferlazzo.edublogs.org/2017/03/23/everyone-is-a-teacher-is-a-new-engagement-strategy-im-using-it-seems-to-be-working

Ferlazzo, L. (2019, July 16). Being a mentor at our school may have resulted in improved grades for the . . . mentors. *Larry Ferlazzo's Website of the Day.* https://larryferlazzo.edublogs.org/2019/07/16/being-a-mentor-at-our-school-may-have-resulted-in-improved-grades-for-the-mentors/

Ferlazzo, L., & Hull-Sypnieski, K. (2022). *The ESL/ELL teacher's survival guide: Ready-to- use strategies, tools, and activities for teaching English language learners of all levels* (2nd edition). Jossey-Bass.

Fletcher-Wood, H. (2019, March 24). Motivating students: Setting goals for autonomy and competence. *Improving Teaching.* https://improvingteaching.co.uk/2019/03/24/motivating-students-setting-goals-for-autonomy-and-competence/

Herrera, T. (2018, December 2). Hide your phone when you're trying to work. Seriously. *The New York Times.* www.nytimes.com/2018/12/02/smarter-living/be-more-productive-hide-your-phone.html

Jones, V. F. (2015). *Practical classroom management.* Pearson Education.

Kahne, J., Bowyer, B., Marshall, J., & Hodgin, E. (2022). Is responsiveness to student voice related to academic outcomes? Strengthening the rationale for student voice in school reform. *American Journal of Education, 128*(3), 389–415. https://doi.org/10.1086/719121

Katz, I., & Assor, A. (2007). When choice motivates and when it does not. *Educational Psychology Review, 19*(4), 429–442. https://doi.org/10.1007/s10648-006-9027-y

Keller, V., & Webb, C. (2017, March 8). Find purpose in even your most mundane tasks at work. *Harvard Business Review.* https://hbr.org/2017/03/find-purpose-in-even-your-most-mundane-tasks-at-work

McQuillan, J. (2017, October 12). A trial of tiers: Why silent reading beats other "tier 1" interventions all day long. *The Backseat Linguist.* https://backseatlinguist.com/blog/a-trial-of-tiers-why-silent-reading-beats-other-tier-1-interventions-all-day-long/

Murphy, B. Jr. (2020, November 1). Google says it still uses the "20-percent rule," and you should totally copy it. *Inc.* www.inc.com/bill-murphy-jr/google-says-it-still-uses-20-percent-rule-you-should-totally-copy-it.html

NASEM et al. (2018). *How people learn II: Learners, contexts, and cultures.* National Academies of Sciences, Engineering and Medicine, Board on Behavioral, Cognitive and Sensory Sciences, Board on Science Education, & Committee on How People Learn II: The Science and Practice of Learning.

Obeidat, M., & Alomari, M. A. (2020). The effect of inductive and deductive teaching on efl undergraduates' achievement in grammar at the Hashemite University in Jordan. *International Journal of Higher Education,* 9(2), 280. https://doi.org/10.5430/ijhe.v9n2p280

Online Etymology Dictionary. (2017, May 11). Agency (n.). www.etymonline.com/word/agency?ref=etymonline_crossreference

Panadero, E., Jonsson, A., & Botella, J. (2017). Effects of self-assessment on self-regulated learning and self-efficacy: Four meta-analyses. *Educational Research Review,* 22, 74–98. https://doi.org/10.1016/j.edurev.2017.08.004

Phillips, K. W. (2014, October 1). How diversity makes us smarter. *Scientific American.* www.scientific american.com/article/how-diversity-makes-us-smarter/

Prince, M. J., & Felder, R. M. (2006). Inductive teaching and learning methods: Definitions, comparisons, and research bases. *Journal of Engineering Education,* 95(2), 123–138. https://doi.org/10.1002/j.2168-9830.2006. tb00884.x

Resnick, B. (2020, January 2). Why willpower is overrated. *Vox.* www.vox.com/science-and-health/2018/ 1/15/16863374/willpower-overrated-self-control-psy chology

Schwartz, K. (2016, January 11). Research-based strategies to help children develop self-control. *Mind/Shift.* www. kqed.org/mindshift/43326/research-based-strategies-to-help-children-develop-self-control

Scott, J. (2021, September 23). Student perceptions on teaching: Can student surveys provide useful feedback for teacher learning? *Evidence Based Education.* https://evidencebased.education/student-surveys-perceptions-on-teaching/

Shafer, L. (2018, January 17). Learning to self manage. www.gse.harvard.edu/news/uk/18/01/learning-self-manage

Sparks, S. D. (2012, May 15). Studies on multitasking highlight value of self-control. *Education Week*. www.edweek.org/leadership/studies-on-multitasking-highlight-value-of-self-control/2012/05

Sparks, S. D. (2022, April 24). 3 counterintuitive findings about motivation that teachers can use. *Education Week*. www.edweek.org/teaching-learning/3-counterintuitive-findings-about-motivation-that-teachers-can-use/2022/04

Stefanou, C. R., Perencevich, K. C., DiCintio, M., & Turner, J. C. (2004). Supporting autonomy in the classroom: Ways teachers encourage student decision making and ownership. *Educational Psychologist*, *39*(2), 97–110. https://doi.org/10.1207/s15326985ep3902_2

Strauss, V. (2019, January 18). News break (not breaking news): Teacher asks students to grade him. www.washingtonpost.com/education/2019/01/18/news-break-not-breaking-news-teacher-asks-students-grade-him-one-wrote-i-give-mr-ferlazzo-an-being-annoying

Terada, Y. (2021, February 21). New research makes a powerful case for PBL. *Edutopia*. www.edutopia.org/article/new-research-makes-powerful-case-pbl

Thibodeaux, W. (2022). Your performance goes up when you do this 1 odd thing, study finds. *Inc.* www.inc.com/wanda-thibodeaux/your-performance-goes-up-when-you-do-this-1-odd-thing-study-finds.html

Toppo, G. (2018, June 6). Softening claims of the marshmallow test. *Inside Higher Ed.* www.insidehighered.com/news/2018/06/06/new-findings-cast-doubt-marshmallow-test-success-claims

Trescott, J. (2011, August 24). Music of the movement: Eyes on the prize. *The Washington Post*. www.washingtonpost.com/blogs/arts-post/post/music-of-the-movement-eyes-on-the-prize/2011/08/03/gIQAuLqbZJ_blog.html

Yew, E. H. J., & Goh, K. (2016). Problem-based learning: An overview of its process and impact on learning. *Health Professions Education*, *2*(2), 75–79. https://doi.org/10.1016/j.hpe.2016.01.004.

3   What Is "Competence" and Why Is it Important?

Competence means feeling like you have the skills and abilities to successfully complete a task, especially if you think the task is not a particularly easy one. Also called self-efficacy (Bandura, 1977), some researchers suggest that—of the multiple elements discussed in this book needed to activate an intrinsic motivation to learn—it is the most important one (Barshay, 2021).

Albert Bandura developed self-efficacy theory, which states that in addition to past experiences of success (or failure), there are three other main elements that influence our sense of self-efficacy: if we see others like ourselves being successful, or having had success in the past, with similar tasks; if we receive supportive feedback while we are working on the task and afterwards; and if we are in a healthy psychological state, and have strong mechanisms to deal with stress and anxiety (Durrington Research School Team, 2017; Lopez-Garrido, 2020).

The strategies listed in this chapter have the potential of positively impacting all four of those "influences" on our students. How likely is it that many of us would feel motivated to do something if we felt we would be unsuccessful doing it? Perhaps we can

DOI: 10.4324/9781315208824-3   **65**

begin to help our students build and expand the self-confidence and the skills they need to be successful.

What Are Ways Teachers Can Support Students' Sense of Competence?

15. Helping Students Develop a Growth Mindset

Researcher Carol Dweck originally developed the growth mindset concept, which suggests that struggle is a natural part of learning, and that we have the potential to learn most things through effort—overcoming obstacles is just part of the process. A growth mindset perspective views mistakes as opportunities to learn. Having a growth mindset might not mean we believe we can become Nobel Prize winners or professional athletes, but it does mean we can get better and make progress (McQuaid, 2017). Dr. Dweck contrasts this possibility with a fixed mindset, which can mean you believe that struggling to learn indicates you might not be "naturally" smart enough to succeed. Having that perspective may result in you avoiding challenges or being discouraged by them (Glei, 2020). If you have a fixed mindset, you might be afraid of making mistakes because making them may not make you look "smart."

Multiple studies have found that having a growth mindset can boost intrinsic motivation (Ng, 2018; Tomlinson & Sousa, 2020), as well as improve academic achievement (OECD, 2021; Porter et al., 2022; Yeager et al., 2019). Having a growth mindset is sometimes characterized as "The Power of Yet," as in "I just haven't learned _____, yet" (Dweck, 2014).

Just as we can be motivated by both intrinsic and extrinsic motivation at times, though, the same can be true with a growth mindset—sometimes we may have a growth mindset, depending on how we are feeling that day and what we are doing, and sometimes we might have a fixed mindset (Hattie, 2017). It's more of a question of which one we tend to have and which tends to guide our actions.

Recently, Dr. Dweck and others have spoken about "false growth mindsets" (Gross-Loh, 2016). They critique some who praise all student effort unconditionally, instead of focusing on praising specific effort that is productive (see more recommendations on providing feedback to students later in this chapter), and offering new helpful strategies to assist students in moving forward. We teachers can't just blame a student's lack of progress on their having a fixed mindset (Killian, 2020). Dr. Dweck does not specifically highlight in her definition of a false growth mindset the fact that societal equity issues like racism and poverty can also impact how far someone might be able to take this belief. It is nevertheless important for teachers to understand, and communicate to students, that a growth mindset is important, but it is not a cure all for everything (Strauss, 2014).

Here is a simple lesson I use to introduce a growth mindset to my students:

1. I first begin by providing a definition of a growth mindset. I ask students what "grow" means, and then what "mind" means. I continue by explaining it means to grow our mind by looking at problems as just another thing to get through, and not to feel stopped by them—they are opportunities to "grow our mind."

2. Next, I share a few short video clips from movies, cartoons and television shows demonstrating examples of a growth mindset (see the EdTech Support Box for links to them). After each one,

I have students think for a moment about what the video clip might be saying about what a growth mindset means and ask students to share their ideas with a partner, and then some tell the class. We make a continuing list on the board or document camera.

3. I then distribute, and read aloud, three stories in Figure 3.1 showing a growth mindset. I explain that as I read them, students should be thinking of their own examples since they will be writing them next.

4. Next, I give students the writing frame in Figure 3.2. I ask them to think about what we wrote on the easel paper/document camera about the elements of a growth mindset and try to remember a time when they may have acted like they had one. We go through each section one-at-a-time, and then students copy them down into a paragraph. Students then share their paragraphs in a "speed-dating" process where they move from desk-to-desk.

This kind of introductory lesson creates an understanding and a vocabulary that can then be used regularly during the school year.

What Is "Competence" and Why Is it Important?

From Mr. Ferlazzo:	I have shown a growth mindset here at school. Last year, I taught a very bad lesson on writing a story. Students didn't really know what I was talking about, and I didn't provide them enough support. I was very disappointed in myself. I could have just moved on to the next lesson and forgotten about my mistake. Instead, that night I spent time thinking about what I did wrong and what I could do better. I made a new lesson. The next day, I apologized to the class and I taught students how to write a story in a much better way. Everybody learned how to write a story. I felt better because I learned from my mistake and did a better job.
From Others:	I have been able to show a growth mindset. When I came to the United States, I didn't speak that much English. I was afraid to speak English. My friends didn't understand me. Then I started reading books in English and working harder in English class. I didn't give up. My friends began to understand what I was talking about, and that made me feel happy. That's how I learned English.
	I showed a growth mindset at home. I was trying to learn how to change a transmission on a car. My dad was trying to teach me, but I was getting frustrated because I couldn't get it right. That night, I tried to remember everything my father had shown me and replayed it in my mind. The next day, I tried again. I remembered what I did wrong before. I learned how to do it. I didn't give up the first time. Now I can do it on my own. I feel successful.

Figure 3.1 Growth mindset stories.

What Is "Competence" and Why Is it Important?

Name:	
	My Growth Mindset Story
Topic Sentence:	I have shown a growth mindset at (school, home, playing sports, etc.)
The Problem:	
How the problem affected me and made me feel:	
What action I took to show a growth mindset:	
How showing a growth mindset made me feel:	
Now, put it all together into one paragraph:	

Figure 3.2   Growth mindset story frame.

Another way researchers have found to support student development of a growth mindset is by teaching about the malleability of the brain (Sparks, 2018). In other words, this concept helps students understand that intelligence is not fixed and that our brain actually changes as we learn.

There is a lesson plan teaching about brain malleability in one of my previous books, *Helping Students Motivate Themselves* (Ferlazzo, 2011, p. 14). I have also done a more simple version of it. You, too, could do this version by first searching online using the phrases "you can grow your intelligence," "you can grow your brain," or "teaching students their brain is like a muscle." Any of them will lead you to many accessible articles and videos (or you can find similar resources at links in the EdTech Support Box).

1. I begin the lesson by telling students that we are going to learn about how the brain is like a muscle and that it gets stronger when learning new things.
2. Then, I will either show one of the short videos available online and/or have students read one of the articles about it. I will ask students to engage with the video or text by asking them to write a short summary of what they learned either on their own or with a partner.
3. Next, I have students replicate what one study did and implement what is called the "saying is believing" effect by having them craft a letter to a younger person in their life telling them why the brain can grow (Yeager et al., 2013). I offer extra credit if they actually read it to the young person and write about their reaction (for students who don't have easy access to a younger person, I still ask them to write the letter and give them an extra credit option of reading another piece or watching

a different video on the concept and writing a short summary).

This kind of lesson can be done in conjunction with one specifically on a growth mindset or a "stand alone." Either way, it provides a common understanding and vocabulary that can be used in class discussions and individual conversations throughout the year.

EDTECH TOOLBOX

You can find video clips illustrating a growth mindset at "The Best TV/Movie Scenes Demonstrating a 'Growth Mindset'—Help Me Find More" (https://larryferlazzo.edublogs.org/2015/06/30/can-you-help-me-find-tvmovie-scenes-demonstrating-a-growth-mindset/) and more related resources and lesson plans at "The Best Resources on Helping Our Students Develop a 'Growth Mindset'" (https://larryferlazzo.edublogs.org/2012/10/13/the-best-resources-on-helping-our-students-develop-a-growth-mindset/).

You can also find many resources on teaching about the malleability of the brain at "The Best Resources for Showing Students that They Make Their Brain Stronger by Learning" (https://larryferlazzo.edublogs.org/2011/11/26/the-best-resources-for-showing-students-that-they-make-their-brain-stronger-by-learning/).

16. Providing Effective Feedback to Students

We teachers are feedback "machines"—we do it all day long! And there is enough advice—much of it having value—out there on how to give it to fill countless books.

The EdTech Support Box will point you in the direction to find a whole lot of that advice. This section, however, will focus on a few ways that researchers, and I, have used that appear to be particularly effective at enhancing students' sense of competence and also assisting in the development of intrinsic motivation.

Feedback to support a growth mindset needs to focus on praising specific actions and the effort that went into them, including learning strategies that students use; not giving evaluative judgments about what kind of person you think the student might be. In other words, saying, "Wow, Pablo, I was very impressed that you spent the time to write two drafts of the essay, and I saw that you asked Danny to read it and give you suggestions. Revising drafts is key for developing good final completed versions, and your classmates can be a good source for suggestions. It really paid off in an excellent final version" could be promoting a growth mindset because it praised the effort he put into it, the learning strategies he used, and the fact that he asked for help.

As David Yeager, Gregory Walton and Geoffrey L. Cohen (2013, p. 65) wrote in their article, "Addressing Achieving Gaps with Psychological Interventions": "Effective growth mindset interventions challenge the myth that raw ability matters most by teaching the fuller formula for success: effort + strategies + help from others."

Saying, "Wow, Mary, I loved your essay. You're a great writer!" could be supporting a fixed mindset. In Mary's example, you are emphasizing the outcome and not acknowledging the process that went into it.

According to Dweck, Pablo could be more inclined in the future to believe he is more likely to be successful if he works hard at something, is conscious of applying learning strategies, and is not afraid of asking for help. Mary, on the other hand, might be more inclined to think she's naturally an excellent writer, perhaps doesn't need to work as hard at it, and might be discouraged if her next essay is not as good.

Of course, these two examples are a bit of an exaggeration—it's unlikely one piece of feedback is going to set a student on a life-long path towards a growth or fixed mindset. However, a school year's worth of teacher commentary could have a substantial impact on how students see themselves.

When trying to remember "in the moment" about what kind of feedback to give to students, it might be helpful to think of this guideline: *describe and/or question* (Ferlazzo, 2011, p. 69). Here are examples of praise using that model and which might promote a growth mindset:

- "Johnny, it was impressive that you did three drafts of the introduction to your essay. Good writers are always trying to make improvements on what they write. What made you want to put that extra effort into it?"
- "It really showed maturity today, Mary, when you asked for help on doing today's project. Some people might feel it's a sign of weakness. I think it shows strength! We all need help sometime and we should be willing to ask for it."
- To a student who might be facing behavior challenges: "Al, you were really focused during the small group activity today. Can you tell me what you did or thought of yourself so you wouldn't be distracted? It would give me some ideas that I could suggest to other students."

This process-praising model might be fairly easy for teachers to remember and do. But what about when we have to give more critical feedback? How can we do that and promote a growth mindset, or at least help ignite some intrinsic motivation?

First, we want to make sure we're looking for opportunities to give much more positive than critical/negative feedback. Research varies on the appropriate ratio—from a positive to critical ratio from 3:1 to 5:1 (Pozen, 2013; Terada, 2021). In my experience, I think just making sure you are conveying more positivity than negativity is sufficient enough. Critical feedback is obviously more likely to be well-received if done in the context of interaction that is generally more positive and if the recipient feels valued (Berinato, 2018).

However, might there also be a way that we can provide critical feedback without the student viewing it as negative or critical?

I think there is, and that's why I'm a big fan of Pixar Studios' feedback strategy called "plussing" (Tugend, 2013). Simply put, "plussing" replaces the words "but" and "no" with "and" and "what if."

So, instead of telling Jackson, "No, this is not an acceptable essay. The outline I gave you clearly laid-out the parts it needed to include, but you're missing several parts. Go back and redo it," we could say, "I like what you have written so far. Let's take a look at the outline I passed out. What if you included much of what you have already written and added these two parts. I think that would make an excellent essay. What do you think?"

When "plussing" doesn't seem to work for the situation, or teachers view it as too much work, some researchers suggest that critical feedback causes the least damage to intrinsic motivation when it includes specific suggestions on how to improve and when it's communicated in person (Fong et al., 2019). Dr. Robert Brooks also suggests that this kind of feedback include a "we" statement like "This strategy you're using doesn't seem to be working. Let's figure out why and how we can change the strategy so that you are successful" (Brooks 2007 as cited in Washburn, 2017, para. 11)

Another strategy, called "wise feedback," has been shown to be particularly effective at enhancing motivation among African American students who may be distrusting of school because of previous experiences (Yeager et al., 2014). This three-step method begins by the teacher communicating high expectations to the student, then conveying faith in the student's ability to achieve those expectations, and next sharing specific feedback on what the student can do to improve (Center for Teaching Innovation, 2021). It could sound something like this:

> Writing an argument essay may be one of the most difficult kinds of essays to write, and being able to do it well will put you in a position of being able to write pretty much anything else you're asked to do. I know you can do it because I have seen the high quality of your writing in the past. I'd like you to look again carefully at the examples of effective claims that I gave the class yesterday and see if you can notice any differences between yours and them. Then, I'd like you to revise what you've written.

One other important point to keep in mind when we consider our feedback strategies: researchers have found that students who are more advanced or skilled tend to be more eager to hear critical feedback than novices (Fishbach, 2022).

Differentiated instruction is discussed later in this chapter as an important strategy for helping our students develop a sense of competence. Being prepared to differentiate our feedback is an important part of that process.

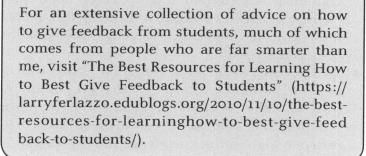

EDTECH TOOLBOX

For an extensive collection of advice on how to give feedback from students, much of which comes from people who are far smarter than me, visit "The Best Resources for Learning How to Best Give Feedback to Students" (https://larryferlazzo.edublogs.org/2010/11/10/the-best-resources-for-learninghow-to-best-give-feedback-to-students/).

17. Emphasizing "Temporal Comparisons"

"Temporal comparisons" are a fancy term to describe when students compare themselves to their past selves instead of to others (Gürel & Brummelman, 2020). In other words, it is about helping students see their own progress, instead of highlighting how they are doing in comparison with others. Temporal comparisons have been shown to be effective in positively impacting students' competence beliefs (Wolff et al., 2020).

There are many ways to support students doing these kinds of "temporal comparisons" in the classroom, including:

● Give students a list of vocabulary terms that they will be using in an upcoming unit and have them check off which ones they know. Collect the sheets, give them back to students at the end of the unit, and ask them to check off the ones they know at that time.

- Have students record themselves reading a text at the beginning of the year (there are many free tools that can be used. Search the Internet for "online recording tools" to find one that isn't blocked by your district's content filters). Then, have them record themselves reading it at times throughout the year to see their improvements in reading fluency and prosody.

- Ask students to keep the essays they write during the year (or teachers keep the essays for them). At the end of the first semester, and at the end of the school year, ask them to rewrite one of their first essays based on the knowledge they've gained in the interim.

- Use *K-W-L charts* (What I Think I Know Now, What I Want to Know, What I've Learned) at the beginning of a unit. Have students first write down in the "what they think they know column," and periodically write what they've learned as the unit progresses.

- Give students several *clozes* ("gap-fill" texts) at the beginning of the year. Then have them complete the same clozes at the end of the first semester and at the end of the year. They will then be able to see the improvement in their scores.

- Similarly, ask students to come up to your desk individually while the rest of the class is working on a project. Have each student read two-or-three different texts for one-minute each and mark-off how many words they read during each minute, and how many errors they made (see the EdTech Support Box for sources of materials). Keep track and show students their improvement during the year.

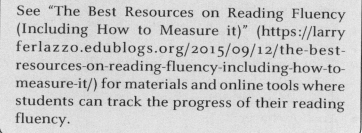

EDTECH TOOLBOX

See "The Best Resources on Reading Fluency (Including How to Measure it)" (https://larry ferlazzo.edublogs.org/2015/09/12/the-best-resources-on-reading-fluency-including-how-to-measure-it/) for materials and online tools where students can track the progress of their reading fluency.

18. Include Adequate Scaffolding during Instruction

The term "scaffolding," used in the context of teaching, was first coined by David Wood, Jerome Bruner, and Gail Ross in 1976. They borrowed the term from the construction industry, where scaffolding refers to a temporary structure that is put into place to support workers until a permanent structure is completed (Wood et al., 1976). In education, scaffolds are tools designed to help students successfully complete tasks in a step-by-step process that might be just out of their reach without that kind of assistance. This kind of progress subsequently enhances intrinsic student motivation "through increasing their expectancies for success" (Belland et al., 2013). Once they gain knowledge and skill with that support, the idea is that they will be able to do it in the future without those "scaffolds."

Scaffolds can include, but are not limited to:

- Sentence starters and sentence frames
- Writing frames (basically longer sentence frames)

- Graphic organizers
- Activating background knowledge
- Think alouds
- Cooperative and collaborative learning
- Pre-teaching vocabulary words that will be used in upcoming lessons
- Teacher modeling of activities
- Visual aids
- "Text engineering"—making complex text more accessible through added white space, images, vocabulary definitions, etc.
- Anchor charts
- The gradual release of responsibility model: "I do it," "We do it," "You do it together," and "You do it alone" via Douglas Fisher (2008). I like to add a fifth step—"You teach it."

Figure 3.3 is an example of a scaffold to help students write a short paragraph to answer a question.

What Is "Competence" and Why Is it Important?

Answer the question using the ABC format:	Example: Do you think Lionel Messi is better than Ronaldo?	Now it's your turn: Do you think we should celebrate Columbus Day?
Answer the question:	I think Lionel Messi is better than Ronaldo. He is the best football player in the world.	I do think we should celebrate Columbus Day OR I do not think we should celebrate Columbus Day.
"Back it up" with information from the article and presentations	They have both scored about the same number of goals, but Messi's team has won more championships.	The article and presentation said:

Figure 3.3 Writing frame for an ABC paragraph.

What Is "Competence" and Why Is it Important?

Comment on how the information supports your answer	A great player makes the people around you great. Messi has helped his teammates be greater and won championships.	This supports my answer because:
Now, put it all together in one paragraph	I think Lionel Messi is better than Ronaldo. He is the best football player in the world. They have both scored about the same number of goals, but Messi's team has won more championships. A great player makes the people around you great. Messi has helped his teammates be greater and won championships.	

Figure 3.3 Continued

Just as in the scaffolding used in building construction, teaching scaffolds are designed to be temporary so that students don't become "dependent" on them. The vast majority of scaffolds are tools to support students until they become skilled at the learning task, and then can be removed.

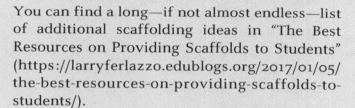

EDTECH TOOLBOX

You can find a long—if not almost endless—list of additional scaffolding ideas in "The Best Resources on Providing Scaffolds to Students" (https://larryferlazzo.edublogs.org/2017/01/05/the-best-resources-on-providing-scaffolds-to-students/).

19. Differentiating Instruction

Scaffolding and differentiating instruction are terms that are often used interchangeably, and many times it is also difficult, if not impossible, to distinguish between the two in classroom practice.

Nevertheless, there are some important ways to tell them apart. Scaffolding often refers to building blocks integrated in advance into a classroom lesson designed to support all students in the learning task. Many times, teachers will "break-up" lessons into specific parts, with many or all parts supported by a specific scaffolding strategy or tool.

Differentiation, on the other hand, often refers to designing a lesson, or making a determination in the moment, to adjust a lesson for certain members of the class in order to make it more accessible to them (Keeling, 2021; Lombardi, 2018).

For example, differentiation strategies could include:

- Using tutors to help specific students.
- Previewing a lesson to one or more ELL students by giving them an article or video in their home language ahead time, and/or having them able to watch a video on their Chromebook with captions in their home language.
- Providing different students with different readings, or a similar reading at a different Lexile level, or share the content on a video.
- Giving a student who appears to be less engaged the option to choose a different essay topic, though it may still be in the same genre that is being taught.
- Providing students different options—and having them propose their own ideas—for working on an activity (alone or in a small group) and presenting their finished project (poster, slideshow, video, etc.).

One way to think about the concept is how Carol Ann Tomlinson characterizes it: Differentiation can be looked at often through the lens of providing student accessible choices through content, process, or product (Ferlazzo, 2014):

- Content: Are there different kinds of materials that provide the essential lesson content in accessible ways?
- Process: Are there different ways that students can do the essential work?
- Product: Are there different ways students can show what they've learned?

Differentiation, like scaffolding, has been shown to help create the conditions for increased student intrinsic motivation, largely because it increases the odds of student success and subsequent feelings of competence (Fenner et al., 2010; Haelermans, 2022; Martin & Pickett, 2013).

EDTECH TOOLBOX

Many more ideas for differentiating instruction can be found at "The Best Resources on Differentiating Instruction" (https://larryferla zzo.edublogs.org/2012/01/09/the-best-resources-on-differentiating-instruction/).

20. Set Up "Fixed Fights"

The term "fixed fights" is used in community organizing to describe easy "wins" that an organization can focus on to build self-confidence among its leaders, public credibility, and community improvement. They usually focus on a smaller community problem that can be quickly solved by negotiating with a public official who is known to be sympathetic to the group.

A similar strategy has been found to positively impact students' sense of self-efficacy in school. In one experiment, some students were given much easier problems to solve than another group. According to researchers, that difference resulted in increased self-efficacy feelings for those in the first group, and those feelings lasted for as long as one year (Uchida et al., 2018).

This kind of activity can be applied to an entire class, or to individual students.

One year, I taught a support class for *Long-Term English Language Learners* (LTELLs)—students who have been a designated ELL for six years or longer (Ferlazzo, 2019). Many LTELLs are very knowledgeable about content, but don't necessarily have the English skills or the self-confidence to communicate what they know. Because of that, they are sometimes not viewed as "smart" students by their teachers or their peers.

My students' content teachers would tell me a week ahead of time what they were going to be covering in their class, and what prior knowledge would be helpful for the students to know. We would then have lessons about that content ahead of time in my class. As a result, they went from their previous many years' experience of not being viewed as "smart" to knowing, and being able to communicate, more about the topic than other students in their content class.

There are obviously many ways to create these kinds of "fixed fights" for individual students, ranging from giving a student who you believe has low self-efficacy a text and companion question/answer exercise that you know is well within a Lexile level they can comprehend (though not too low a level—most students can see through "acts of charity") to doing the same with a group of math problems.

The idea, of course, is not to stay at the "fixed fight" level for long and, instead, use the self-efficacy it builds to quickly move the student to more challenging tasks.

21. Helping Students Develop Strategies to Deal with Stress

As explained earlier, being in a healthy emotional state and knowing effective strategies to deal with stress and anxiety are important for having a sense of self-efficacy. Being preoccupied with these negative emotions does not help us develop self-confidence or support motivation to learn, or to do just about anything (American Addiction Centers, n.d.). On the other hand, developing strategies to better cope with stress can lead to an increased sense of self-efficacy (Freire et al., 2020).

Teachers need to remember that most of us are not mental health professionals, and we should not hesitate to connect our students with school counselors and other outside-of-class assistance. Nevertheless, there are some relatively simple research-based strategies that we can implement or offer to students as ways they can handle stress in their lives and that may also have multiple other benefits. The next four strategies lay-out practical ways to incorporate that research in the classroom.

These plans can all be helpful in assisting students deal with stress in their lives. However, one of the best ways we can support our students when they are facing this challenge—or just about any other one—is to be ready to listen, be empathetic, and take any actions we can think of to show that we care. Asking "Are you okay?" to a student showing any signs of distress, which includes frustration, distractedness, or actions that might be perceived as "misbehavior" by some can be much more effective than a "Get back to work!" admonition.

22. Self-Affirmation Exercises

Multiple studies (Cohen et al., 2009; Goyer et al., 2017) have shown the value of "self-affirmation exercises." In these short activities done three-to-five times a year (or even less), students "affirm" the values they feel are important to them. As a result, they remind themselves that they are more than their grades and develop greater feelings of self-confidence and reduced stress (Sherman et al., 2021). Researchers have found that they also lead to longer-term increases in academic achievement, especially for students who had been experiencing academic challenges.

I have a complete lesson plan for one of these exercises in one of my earlier books, Helping Students Motivate Themselves (page 42). Here, though, is a short summary. Students are given a list of "values," which can change each time the activity is done. For instance, creativity, religious values, friends, family, etc. (https://larryferlazzo.edublogs.org/2010/02/12/useful-writing-exercise-for-helping-students-develop-self-esteem/). They are asked to circle the one that is most important to them.

They are then asked to think about a specific time when the circled value was important and write a few sentences about it: When was that time? What was happening? Why was it important to you then?

Finally, students are given three phrases:

- "This value has influenced my life."
- "In general, I try to live up to this value."
- "This value is an important part of who I am."

They are asked to write one of five ratings next to each one—Very Strongly Agree, Strongly Agree, Agree, Strongly Disagree, or Very Strongly Disagree.

Students can then share their responses in small groups and/or with the entire class.

In the second, third, fourth, and/or fifth times, researchers made minor changes such as giving a different list of values, having students circle more than one value, and/or asking students to write about which values might be most important during a certain time period, like Winter Break.

23. Writing about Good Things that Happened during the Day and/or Expressing Gratitude

Researchers have found that writing down at the end of the day three things that had gone well in the preceding hours resulted in a substantial reduction in feelings of stress (Bono et al., 2013). Offering it as a suggestion to students, or even making it an "extra credit" homework assignment (or a regular one) are ideas worth considering. I've also sometimes had students do it as an every Friday reflection activity, as well as just ask an individual student who was having a difficult time in their life to just do it once or twice. Students have reported to me that they had positive experiences in all of these versions.

Other studies have found that a similar exercise where people write about something they are feeling grateful for each day (Fekete & Deichert, 2022) or even far less often (Allen, 2018) had a similar effect on stress reduction. During some years I've had students doing this kind of reflective exercise alternate between writing about what went well that week and what they are grateful for. Inviting students to periodically share with classmates what they wrote seems to also have the added benefit of developing a greater sense of community within the classroom.

24. Coping with Stress Lesson Plan

There is a four-day lesson plan on helping students develop coping skills for stress in my book, *Self-Driven Learning* (Ferlazzo, 2013, p. 82). The materials for that lesson can be downloaded free at the publisher's website (www.routledge.com/Self-Driven-Learning-Teaching-Strategies-for-Student-Motivation/Ferlazzo/p/book/9781596672390).

25. Inviting Ideas from Students and Visualization

There are two other stress-reduction strategies I've either applied in the classroom or offered individually to students.

The first strategy involves asking students to share how they have successfully dealt with stress as I write their ideas on the whiteboard or document camera. I then encourage them to try new ideas they learn from the list (obviously, I am conscious of any unhealthy or dangerous strategies that might be shared, though that has never happened).

Another strategy is visualization, which I often use to help students see themselves complete challenging tasks, but periodically also include stress reduction guidance (see the EdTech Support Tool Box for more information.

EDTECH TOOLBOX

For more ideas on how to help students develop better stress coping skills, go to "The Best Resources for Learning about Teens & Stress" (https://larryferlazzo.edublogs.org/2011/06/19/the-best-resources-for-learning-about-teens-stress/). For information on visualization activities, see "The Best Posts on Helping Students 'Visualize Success'" (https://larryferlazzo.edublogs.org/2010/12/23/my-best-posts-on-helping-students-visualize-success/).

26. Learning about Role Models

Dr. Bandura's model of self-efficacy also highlights the importance of seeing role models who are or who have been successful. These role models can serve three motivational purposes: "acting as behavioral models, representing the possible, and being inspirational" (Morgenroth et al., 2015).

This model suggests that the more similarities you see in a potential role model, the greater sense of motivation you are likely to feel (Bandura, 1977).

The next strategy highlights how students can utilize this kind of "social modeling" through reading about the "struggle stories" of others and writing their own.

In addition, though, teachers themselves can enhance the likelihood that they can be motivational role models for at least some of their students. Researchers suggest that "shared group membership" (Morgenroth et al., 2015, p. 478) is one characteristic of this kind of effective role model, which speaks to the importance of having teachers who look like their students and highlights the need to recruit and provide ongoing support to teachers of color (Ferlazzo, 2017).

All teachers, however, can try to connect to "common ground" with their students by sharing appropriate stories of struggles, successes, losses and joys. For example, it's not uncommon for me to share during suitable class situations about the deaths of my father when I was a teenager, as well as the death of my first wife. I also share more light-hearted stories about my lifetime as a mediocre basketball player.

"Over-sharing" can be inappropriate and inauthentic. But choosing the right times, with the right tones, to tell students about our lives can strengthen relationships and increase the odds that some students might view us as motivational role models.

27. Struggle Story

This section will offer two ways to approach the concept of role models in class: explicitly teaching about "struggle stories" from potential role models that highlight multiple challenges they faced in their lives and how they overcame them; and reading advice about specific school and school-age -related challenges faced by potential role models who are also students. The second area also offers an opportunity for students to become role-models themselves.

Researchers had students read short (a few hundred words, at most) stories documenting the school, personal, and professional struggles of famous scientists who overcame them. Students then shared if there were any ways they felt connected to those scientist's stories. This activity helped students increase their growth mindset and their academic achievement (Du et al., 2021; Lin-Siegler et al., 2016). Another study suggests that this kind of intervention might be even more successful when sharing "struggle stories" from people who are not as well-known because it is less likely that students will attribute natural "talent" as the reason for their success (Hu et al., 2020).

The researchers wrote the "struggle stories" they used in those studies, and they are not publicly available. I have been able to find only two online sites where similar essays are collected, and another that shares short videos (see the links in the EdTech Support Box). However, I prefer to apply this idea by having my students choose people they want to write about and write their own "struggle stories."

These, in turn, are shared in class and students write about which, if any, they "connect to" and we discuss their reactions.

I tell students that they can write about someone in their family, someone they know, a well-known person, or someone who is not well known but whom they have read or heard about. Figure 3.4 shares one I wrote about my father that students use as a model, and Figure 3.5 is the blank outline that students complete.

What Is "Competence" and Why Is it Important?

	Mr. Ferlazzo's example
Who is the person?	My father.
Why do you consider this person successful?	I consider him successful because he was committed to leaving the world a better place than when he entered it. He was a loving parent, helped many extended family members (including helping some get jobs, and getting others out of jail), and was always in a good mood. He graduated from college, worked hard and provided a comfortable life for us. He taught English to new immigrants who entered the United States. He spoke many languages, and was respected in the community.
Why did you decide to write about this person?	Because he overcame many struggles to be successful, and had a huge positive impact on my life.

Figure 3.4 Struggle story model.

What Is "Competence" and Why Is it Important?

What are some struggles this person had in their life that they had to overcome to become successful? Ideally, you can write about at least one in each area (you will receive extra credit if you can't learn about one struggle in one area, please write about two in another area.

School Struggles: He came to the United States from Italy as a young boy. He didn't speak English, and the schools in the New York City slums were not known for providing a high-quality education. Teachers would punish him if he spoke Italian with his classmates, and he did not do well at school for his first few years. He worked hard, though, and was able to enter one of the top high schools in the city. He learned that with help from his friends and from some teachers who cared, along with his putting in effort, he could realize his dreams.

Personal Struggles: His father walked out on the family, and his mother had to support three young children by working long hours at what was known as a "sweatshop" (a factory with unsafe working conditions that did not pay very well). He worked at part time jobs after school to help support the family. When things got difficult, he always felt that if he just did his best, things would get better—and they generally did.

Figure 3.4 Continued

What Is "Competence" and Why Is it Important?

His brother Horace caused many class disruptions at school. The school staff told his mother about a doctor who could "fix" Horace, and his mother, who did not speak English very well, agreed because she trusted the school. The doctor performed what is called a "lobotomy" on Horace, which meant they removed part of his brain. He could not take care of himself after the operation, and was put in a hospital, where he stayed for the next sixty years. His mother never forgave herself and my father always wondered if there was anything he could have done to prevent it from happening. His mother took the long trip to visit Horace every week, and my father tried to visit him as often as he could. He felt that it was not right that some institutions would take advantage of people because they were poor or because they didn't speak English, and he used that experience to energize him to help people in those situations for the rest of his life.

His marriage was an unhappy one. In spite of that, he was always a loving and caring father, and was always there for his children. He felt that even though parts of his life did not go the way he wanted, he tried to not let it affect the parts that he felt were important and gave him joy, especially his children.

Figure 3.4 Continued

	Professional Struggles: After the war, he struggled to support his new family and continue his education. It took him years of working at a job during the day and going to school at night, but he was finally after to complete his degrees and was able to get a job teaching at a university. However, he didn't feel like he was paid enough money to be able to support a family. Even though he loved teaching, he left the college to work for a private company. Eventually, he decided he had made a mistake by leaving teaching—he missed it so much! So, he started to go to school at night again. This time, though, he wasn't a student—he was the teacher!
What lessons do you think this person's life teaches us?	Even though life can be a struggle, and terrible things can happen to us and our families, it's possible to persevere and be successful in school and professionally, build a good life, and make the world a better place.
How do you connect to this person:	I connect to him because he was able to keep going forward even though he faced many challenges, and he was always still able to be there for others through it all. I try to do the same, though I'm not as successful at doing it as he was.

Figure 3.4 Continued

What Is "Competence" and Why Is it Important?

Name:	
Who is the person?	
Why do you consider this person successful?	
Why did you decide to write about this person?	
What are some struggles this person had in their life that they had to overcome to become successful? Ideally, you can write about at least one in each area (you will receive extra credit if you write more). If you can't learn about one struggle in one area, please write about two in another area.	**School Struggles:** **Personal Struggles:** **Professional Struggles:**
What lessons do you think this person's life teaches us?	
How do you connect to this person:	

Figure 3.5 Struggle story outline.

28. Reading and Reacting to Student-Written Advice about Specific Challenges

Several researchers have done experiments focused on more specific challenges often faced by students in a school environment (generally on a college level) and had them read essays actually or supposedly written by other students who had faced—and overcome—similar problems. As in the previous activity, readers then typically shared their reactions and connections to those stories. Increased academic achievement and psychological well-being were a few of the many positive common results of these interventions (Brady et al., 2020).

There are several online sources of youth-written accessible essays that share stories of overcoming school-related challenges. Teachers can select appropriate essays from there (ones on self-control, anxiety around grades or relationships, etc.) and have students respond to them (see the EdTech Support Box for links).

A related lesson plan can be found in one of my previous books, *Self-Motivated Learners* (Ferlazzo, 2015a, p. 75).

In my view, a particularly effective "extension" activity is to then have students think about a problem they have overcome and then use the online articles as models to write very short essays about them. I also provide a simple outline for students to use if they find it helpful:

1. What was the problem?
2. How was it resolved?
3. What were the steps involved in getting it resolved, including the challenges and how they were overcome?
4. What did you learn from the experience?

Not only does this create a writing opportunity for students, but then, assuming you receive permission from your students, you can keep the best essays for your future students to read (and, with their added permission, even submit them to those online sites for publication!).

EDTECH TOOLBOX

The only two online sites that I have found with longer "struggle stories" written by potential role models in the form of short essays are the "We Are America Project" (www.weareameri caproject.com/) and "I Learn America" (https:// ilearnamerica.com/human-library/). Green Card Voices (www.greencardvoices.org/) collects similar videos, which could be used as models for students to create their own multimedia versions.

Youth-written essays about responding to school-related struggles can be found at "Stage Of Life" (www.stageoflife.com/teen_ challenges.aspx); Youth Today (https://youth today.org/category/youth-voices/#); and Youth Communication (https://youthcomm.org/youth-voice-page/).

29. Creating Opportunities for Students to Teach their Classmates

"Learning by teaching" describes putting students into situations where they have to learn something new, prepare to teach it to others, and then actually teach it. Not only have multiple studies demonstrated that both the "teachers" and the "students" improve their academic achievement (Nestojko et al., 2014; Sparks, 2015), but the activity also increases the self-confidence and sense of self-efficacy among the "teachers" (Stock, 2019).

30. Jigsaws

These "learning by teaching" activities can take many forms (including the "Genius Hours" that were listed earlier in the previous chapter). Here, I'll focus on the Jigsaw strategy, which educational researchers John Hattie and Gregory Donoghue suggest may be the only teaching method that works across what they describe as the four "learning quadrants" where students can initially "acquire" knowledge and then move it to "consolidating deep learning" (Schwartz, 2017). Though there is some criticism about how Professor Hattie develops "effect sizes" for instructional strategies to measure their impact on student learning (Slavin, 2018) it is nevertheless notable that in his analysis, he finds that the jigsaw method has a three-times higher effect size than the average of the many other strategies he reviews (Fisher & Frey, 2018).

What is the jigsaw method? Here are the various versions I use (and I'm sure that there are many other ones used by other teachers), depending on my goals and the time available. It's probably safe to say that a higher level of "consolidating deep learning" would most likely occur in the second and third version, but all apply the "learning by teaching" model.

Version One:

1. The teacher divides up an article or textbook chapter into sections, or perhaps they are different complete articles or videos on a component of a common topic.

2. The class is then divided into small groups (sometimes strategically as a differentiation strategy with some groups getting "easier" sections and others more challenging text; other times randomly through "numbering off").

3. Each small group is assigned a section or article to read together (perhaps by taking turns reading a paragraph aloud while the rest of the group follows along) or a video to watch, and then prepare a poster or slideshow presentation using guidelines given by the teacher (What were the three main points? What was a phrase or sentence that "struck" you and why did it strike you? What is a question you have about the reading?). Note: sometimes I share the list of articles and videos and give each small group a minute to decide on their top two choices, and try to accommodate their wishes.

4. The small groups then present to the entire class.

5. The audience might have an assignment to do as they listen to each group, such as "Write down the most important thing you heard and why you think it is important."

Version Two:

1. The teacher divides up an article or textbook chapter into sections, or perhaps they are complete articles or videos on a component of a common topic.

2. The class is then divided into small groups (sometimes strategically as a differentiation strategy with some groups getting "easier" sections and others more challenging text; other times randomly through "numbering off"). However, they do not read the text together. Instead, students read it individually (generally staying in their

seat), and jot down "rough" notes answering the questions in the presentation guidelines given by the teacher.

3. The students who read the same text then meet together (if there are large numbers of students reading the same text, then they can be divided into groups of three, four, or five).

4. Students in each of these "expert" groups share what they jotted down in response to the teacher's questions about the article. The group might then create a common slideshow presentation consolidating what the group thinks are the best responses or decide to make individual presentations or posters teaching the text using ideas shared in the group discussion (this could be a group or a teacher decision). While this group is meeting, the teacher goes around assigning letters to each student in each of these "expert" groups. These "letter" groups consist of one person from each of the "expert" groups.

5. The "letter" groups meet, and students make individual presentations using the group-created slideshow or the individually made slideshow or poster.

6. The audience might have an assignment they need to do after each presentation, such as writing down what they thought was the most important point that was made. Or, perhaps, they might be assigned to ask a question from a list of Bloom's Taxonomy question-starters.

7. Members of the "letter" group might also have an individual assignment they need to complete after all the presentations are made, such as stating their opinion on the topic and providing evidence from one of the presentations to support their claim, which they would share with partners after

everyone returned to their regular class seats. Or, perhaps the entire "letter" group has a question they have to answer and be prepared to report back to the entire class.

Version Three:

- This version can follow most of the steps in either Versions One or Two. The difference, though, is that students are not given sections of a specific article, an article, or a video to review. Instead, they are assigned a part of a concept or topic and have to research it before following the steps in the previous versions.
- For example, if the focus is the biography of someone, the sections could be Childhood, Family, Significant Events, Accomplishments, Challenges. Or, the jigsaw could be about the Scientific Method, and the jigsaw parts could be its steps.

In addition to Jigsaws, a multi-day lesson plan on helping students design a "unit" that they teach can be found in one my previous books, *Helping Students Motivate Themselves* (Ferlazzo, 2011, p. 106).

EDTECH TOOLBOX

For additional resources on "learning by teaching," you can visit "The Best Posts on Helping Students Teach Their Classmates— Help Me Find More" (https://larryferlazzo.edu blogs.org/2012/04/22/the-best-posts-on-helping-students-teach-their-classmates-help-me-find-more/).

31. Promoting Positive Self-Talk

Positive self-talk describes people speaking silently or out loud to themselves as a form of encouragement ("I can do this"). It's been shown to help increase people's self-efficacy and reduce anxiety in a variety of contexts (Haas, 2016; Hatzigeorgiadis et al., 2008, 2009).

I first introduce the idea of positive self-talk by showing a short video of basketball great Stephen Curry using self-talk by telling himself, "I control my own destiny" (Ferlazzo, 2015b).

I explain that researchers have found that saying something encouraging to ourselves before or when we are doing something that might be challenging, or when we are feeling discouraged, often helps us do and feel better. I point out that many athletes do it all the time. Then, I give students a copy of the worksheet found in Figure 3.6, which was created by Centervention (www.centervention.com/practicing-positive-self-talk-worksheet/), an organization that provides online Social Emotional Learning games to schools and students. I point out that students can connect a variety of positive self-talk messages to many of the listed feelings—it doesn't have to be one-to-one, and these are just some examples we can use.

Then I ask students to add their own positive self-talk messages to the list, along when they think it would be helpful. I give an example of my often saying just one word to myself at the beginning of a class: "Patience." It's a reminder for me to show more patience than I sometimes do.

Next, students share what they wrote with a partner if they feel comfortable sharing and ask some students to tell the entire class (again, only if they feel okay doing so).

What Is "Competence" and Why Is it Important?

In some years, I have students make posters sharing their favorite self-talk words or phrases. In other years, students just glue them in their notebooks. For the first few days following this activity, I ask students to review their sheet at the beginning of the class and use it that day. I hope this reminder gets them in the habit of using it. After that, I'll just give a periodic reminder, and hope that at least some students continue with the practice.

What Is "Competence" and Why Is it Important?

Name: _____

Positive Thoughts

Draw a line from each feeling to a positive thought that can help you feel better.

Feeling

When I feel nervous

When I feel frustrated

When I'm disappointed

When someone is mean

When I'm left out

When I feel discouraged

Positive Thought

"I'm going to get better at this."

"I am a great student."

"I can get through anything."

"I get better every single day."

"I have courage and confidence."

"I believe in myself."

"I am proud of myself."

"I am a great friend."

Centervention.

© Centervention, 2019

https://www.centervention.com/

Figure 3.6. Practicing Positive Self Talk Worksheet. Reproduced with permission from Centervention.

> ## EDTECH TOOLBOX
>
> For additional resources on student "self-talk," you can go to "The Best Resources on the Value of Positive 'Self-Talk'" (https://larryferlazzo. edublogs.org/2016/06/30/another-study-finds-that-self-talk-works/).

What Questions Can Teachers Ask Themselves to Ensure Their Strategies To Promote Student Competence Are Also Culturally Responsive?

- Do I publicly acknowledge that there are political and systemic barriers to equal opportunity that need to be challenged, or do I communicate that it just takes a growth mindset and trying harder to accomplish anything my students want?
- When I use any of the suggested methods for feedback that are in this chapter, do I maintain the stance of being what culturally responsive educator and writer Zaretta Hammond calls being a "warm demander" (Kubic, 2021). In other words, do I not shy away from being personally warm and supportive *and* communicating high expectations providing direct guidance?
- Am I making sure that I only use "temporal comparisons" in my classroom and do not compare students to other classmates? Our students are likely doing too much of the latter already on their own, and it's generally not helping them feel or do any better (White et al., 2006).
- When I plan to use "activating background knowledge" as a scaffold for my lessons, do I make sure that I include what are called "cultural scaffolds"

(Pawan, 2008; Stone, 2014) for English Language Learners, which include thinking about how they and I can use their home language and culture to help make sure the lesson content is accessible to them? Though cultural scaffolds are particularly important for ELLs, they can be helpful for all students. Do I spend any time trying to learn about my students' cultures and "social" languages, so I am better able to know about possible cultural scaffolds to incorporate into lessons?

- Do I look for ways to not only help individual students use their other languages and their cultures to access important content, but to also lift up those assets so that all students can learn from them?

- When I create "fixed fights" to help build-up students' self-confidence, am I making sure they are not too easy? It is not uncommon for students of color to have had—and been aware of—mediocre work praised by teachers in misguided attempts to strengthen self-esteem and/or avoid being perceived as prejudiced (Yeager et al., 2014). Badly planned fixed fights can just feed into these feelings of students not feeling respected.

- If I am introducing role models to my students, am I making sure these role models are diverse and that all my students can see themselves in them, including through gender, race, and occupation?

- If I am having students write "struggle stories" about people they choose, am I supportive of those who decide to write about family members who demonstrate important positive qualities, but who might not fit into my definition of a "successful" person? Of course, there are always exceptions to everything, and this does not mean we have to support a student who wants to write about someone who might be doing an illegal activity that is not necessarily beneficial to society (I have a family member who demonstrated many positive qualities worth emulating, but I wouldn't highlight him if he still had his "job" of driving cars into the river so their owners could collect insurance money). But there are many others who are successful, but who might not just fit a white middle-class perception of that category. There's an important caveat to keep in mind—many people have "struggle stories" that may have included illegal activity in the past, but now have persevered beyond it. These kinds of stories could be important ones for our students to write and read.

- Differentiating instruction can often mean making a change in your lesson plan "in the moment." Do I model flexibility by accommodating the needs of students to make my academic content more accessible, or do I tend to be rigid and insist on sticking to the letter of my plans?

- If I see some of my students struggling in academics, do I tend to view their difficulties through the deficit lens of an "achievement gap" and put the primary responsibility for it on the student, or do I tend to view it as an "opportunity gap" and put the primary responsibility on factors that may have been or are outside the student's ability to control them? Do my reactions tend to lead to frustration and complaints, or are they focused more on looking for ways to increase their opportunities?

References

Allen, S. (2018). *The science of gratitude.* Greater Good Science Center. https://ggsc.berkeley.edu/images/upl oads/GGSC-JTF_White_Paper-Gratitude-FINAL.pdf

American Addiction Centers. (n.d.). Self-efficacy and the perception of control in stress reduction. www.mentalhelp.net/stress/self-efficacy-and-the-perception-of-control-in-stress-reduction

Bandura, A. (1977). Self-efficacy: Toward a unifying theory of behavioral change. *Psychological Review*, *84*(2), 191–215.

Barshay, J. (2021, September 27). Proof points: What almost 150 studies say about how to motivate students. *The Hechinger Report*. https://hechingerreport.org/proof-points-what-almost-150-studies-say-about-how-to-motivate-students/

Belland, B. R., Kim, C., & Hannafin, M. J. (2013). A framework for designing scaffolds that improve motivation and cognition. *Educational Psychologist*, *48*(4), 243–270. https://doi.org/10.1080/00461520.2013.838920

Berinato, S. (2018, February). Negative feedback rarely leads to improvement. *Harvard Business Review*. https://hbr.org/2018/01/negative-feedback-rarely-leads-to-improvement

Bono, J. E., Glomb, T. M., Shen, W., Kim, E., & Koch, A. J. (2013). Building positive resources: Effects of positive events and positive reflection on work stress and health. *Academy of Management Journal*, *56*(6), 1601–1627. https://doi.org/10.5465/amj.2011.0272

Brady, S. T., Cohen, G. L., Jarvis, S. N., & Walton, G. M. (2020). A brief social-belonging intervention in college improves adult outcomes for Black Americans. *Science Advances*, *6*(18), eaay3689. https://doi.org/10.1126/sciadv.aay3689

Center for Teaching Innovation. (2021). Wise feedback: Helping students persist. https://elearning.salemstate.edu/courses/1313306/pages/wise-feedback-helping-students-persist

Cohen, G. L., Garcia, J., Purdie-Vaughns, V., Apfel, N., & Brzustoski, P. (2009). Recursive processes in self-affirmation: Intervening to close the minority achievement gap. *Science*, *324*(5925), 400–403. https://doi.org/10.1126/science.1170769

Du, X., Yuan, S., Liu, Y., & Bai, X. (2021). Reading struggle stories of role models can improve students' growth mindsets. *Frontiers in Psychology*, 12, 747039. https://doi.org/10.3389/fpsyg.2021.747039

Durrington Research School Team. (2017, June 18). What is self-efficacy and how can we help our students to get more of it? *Class Teaching*. https://classteaching.wordpress.com/2017/06/18/what-is-self-efficacy-and-how-can-we-help-our-students-to-get-more-of-it/

Dweck, C. S. (Director). (2014, September 12). The power of yet. TEDxNorrköping. www.youtube.com/watch?v=J-swZaKN2Ic

Fekete, E. M., & Deichert, N. T. (2022). A brief gratitude writing intervention decreased stress and negative affect during the COVID-19 pandemic. *Journal of Happiness Studies*, 23(6), 2427–2448. https://doi.org/10.1007/s10902-022-00505-6

Fenner, D., Kayyal Mansour, S., & Sydor, N. (2010). *The effects of differentiation and motivation on students' performance [action research masters project]*. Saint Xavier University. https://eric.ed.gov/?id=ED510605

Ferlazzo, L. (2011). *Helping students motivate themselves: Practical answers to classroom challenges*. Eye on Education.

Ferlazzo, L. (2013). *Self-driven learning: Teaching strategies for student motivation*. Eye on Education.

Ferlazzo, L. (2014, April 18). Response: Differentiating lessons by "content, process, or product." *Education Week Opinion*. www.edweek.org/teaching-learning/opinion-response-differentiating-lessons-by-content-process-or-product/2014/04

Ferlazzo, L. (2015a). *Building a community of self-motivated learners: Strategies to help students thrive in school and beyond*. Routledge.

Ferlazzo, L. (2015b, June 16). "Control your destiny": Positive self-talk, students & Stephen Curry. *Larry Ferlazzo's Website of the Day*. https://larryferlazzo.edublogs.org/2015/06/16/control-your-own-destiny-positive-self-talk-students-stephen-curry/).

Ferlazzo, L. (2017). New & revised: The best resources for understanding why we need more teachers of color. https://larryferlazzo.edublogs.org/2017/12/26/

new-revised-the-best-resources-for-understanding-why-we-need-more-teachers-of-color

Ferlazzo, L. (2019). Research in action: Ramping up support for long-term ells. *Education Leadership, 77*(4). www.ascd.org/el/articles/research-in-action-ramping-up-support-for-long-term-ells

Fishbach, A. (2022). *Get it done: Surprising lessons from the science of motivation* (1st edition). Little, Brown Spark.

Fisher, D. (2008). Effective use of the gradual release of responsibility model. https://srhscollaborationsuite.weebly.com/uploads/3/8/4/0/38407301/douglas_fisher.pdf

Fisher, D., & Frey, N. (2018). Let's get jigsaw right. *Education Leadership, 76*(3). www.ascd.org/el/articles/lets-get-jigsaw-right

Fong, C. J., Patall, E. A., Vasquez, A. C., & Stautberg, S. (2019). A meta-analysis of negative feedback on intrinsic motivation. *Educational Psychology Review, 31*(1), 121–162. https://doi.org/10.1007/s10648-018-9446-6

Freire, C., Ferradás, M. del M., Regueiro, B., Rodríguez, S., Valle, A., & Núñez, J. C. (2020). Coping strategies and self-efficacy in university students: A person-centered approach. *Frontiers in Psychology, 11*, 841. https://doi.org/10.3389/fpsyg.2020.00841

Glei, J. (2020). Talent isn't fixed and other mindsets that lead to greatness. *99u.* https://99u.adobe.com/articles/14379/talent-isnt-fixed-and-other-mindsets-that-lead-to-greatness

Goyer, J. P., Garcia, J., Purdie-Vaughns, V., Binning, K. R., Cook, J. E., Reeves, S. L., Apfel, N., Taborsky-Barba, S., Sherman, D. K., & Cohen, G. L. (2017). Self-affirmation facilitates minority middle schoolers' progress along college trajectories. *Proceedings of the National Academy of Sciences, 114*(29), 7594–7599. https://doi.org/10.1073/pnas.1617923114

Gross-Loh, C. (2016, December 16). How praise became a consolation prize. *The Atlantic.* www.theatlantic.com/education/archive/2016/12/how-praise-became-a-consolation-prize/510845/

Gürel, Ç., & Brummelman, E. (2020). The problem with telling children they're better than others. *Scientific*

American. www.scientificamerican.com/article/the-pro blem-with-telling-children-theyre-better-than-others/

Haas, S. (2016, June 30). Thinking "I can do better" really can improve performance, study finds. *ScienceDaily.* www.sciencedaily.com/releases/2016/06/160630102 038.htm

Haelermans, C. (2022). The effects of group differentiation by students' learning strategies. *Instructional Science,* 50(2), 223–250. https://doi.org/10.1007/s11251-021-09 575-0

Hattie, J. (2017, June 28). Misinterpreting the growth mindset: Why we're doing students a disservice. *Education Week Opinion.* www.edweek.org/education/ opinion-misinterpreting-the-growth-mindset-why- were-doing-students-a-disservice/2017/06

Hatzigeorgiadis, A., Zourbanos, N., Goltsios, C., & Theodorakis, Y. (2008). Investigating the functions of self-talk: The effects of motivational self-talk on self-efficacy and performance in young tennis players. *The Sport Psychologist,* 22(4), 458–471. https://doi.org/ 10.1123/tsp.22.4.458

Hatzigeorgiadis, A., Zourbanos, N., Mpoumpaki, S., & Theodorakis, Y. (2009). Mechanisms underlying the self-talk–performance relationship: The effects of motivational self-talk on self-confidence and anxiety. *Psychology of Sport and Exercise,* 10(1), 186–192. https://doi.org/10.1016/j.psychsport.2008.07.009

Hu, D., Ahn, J. N., Vega, M., & Lin-Siegler, X. (2020). Not all scientists are equal: Role aspirants influence role modeling outcomes in stem. *Basic and Applied Social Psychology,* 42(3), 192–208. https://doi.org/10.1080/019 73533.2020.1734006

Keeling, J. (2021, November 12). Differentiation vs. Scaffolding. *Educators Blog.* www.graduateprogram. org/2020/01/differentiation-vs-scaffolding/

Killian, S. (2020, September 27). False growth mindset explained. *Evidence-Based Teaching.* www.evidence basedteaching.org.au/false-growth-mindset-explained/

Kubic, C. (2021, March 3). Can teachers be warm demanders during the pandemic? *Edutopia.* www. edutopia.org/article/can-teachers-be-warm-demanders- during-pandemic

Lin-Siegler, X., Ahn, J. N., Chen, J., Fang, F.-F. A., & Luna-Lucero, M. (2016). Even Einstein struggled: Effects of learning about great scientists' struggles on high school students' motivation to learn science. *Journal of Educational Psychology, 108*(3), 314–328. https://doi.org/10.1037/edu0000092

Lombardi, P. (2018). *Instructional methods strategies and technologies to meet the needs of all learners.* LibreTexts Project.

Lopez-Garrido, G. (2020, August 9). Self-efficacy theory. *SimplyPsychology.* www.simplypsychology.org/self-efficacy.html

Martin, M., & Pickett, M. (2013). *The effects of differentiation and motivation on students performance [action research masters project].* Saint Xavier University. https://files.eric.ed.gov/fulltext/ED541341.pdf

McQuaid, M. (2017, June 2). Are you getting growth mindset wrong? *Huffpost.* www.huffpost.com/entry/are-you-getting-growth-mindset-wrong_b_59310062e4b0649fff2117d3

Morgenroth, T., Ryan, M. K., & Peters, K. (2015). The motivational theory of role modeling: How role models influence role aspirants' goals. *Review of General Psychology, 19*(4), 465–483. https://doi.org/10.1037/gpr0000059

Nestojko, J. F., Bui, D. C., Kornell, N., & Bjork, E. L. (2014). Expecting to teach enhances learning and organization of knowledge in free recall of text passages. *Memory & Cognition, 42*(7), 1038–1048. https://doi.org/10.3758/s13421-014-0416-z

Ng, B. (2018). The neuroscience of growth mindset and intrinsic motivation. *Brain Sciences, 8*(2), 20. https://doi.org/10.3390/brainsci8020020

OECD. (2021). *Sky's the Limit: Growth mindset, students, and schools in PISA.* OECD.

Pawan, F. (2008). Content-area teachers and scaffolded instruction for English language learners. *Teaching and Teacher Education, 24*(6), 1450–1462. https://doi.org/10.1016/j.tate.2008.02.003

Porter, T., Catalán Molina, D., Cimpian, A., Roberts, S., Fredericks, A., Blackwell, L. S., & Trzesniewski, K. (2022).

Growth-mindset intervention delivered by teachers boosts achievement in early adolescence. *Psychological Science, 33*(7), 1086–1096. https://doi.org/10.1177/0956 7976211061109

Pozen, R. (2013, March 28). The delicate art of giving feedback. *Harvard Business Review*. https://hbr.org/2013/03/the-delicate-art-of-giving-fee

Schwartz, K. (2017, June 14). How do you know when a teaching strategy is most effective? John Hattie has an idea. *Mind/Shift*. www.kqed.org/mindshift/48112/how-do-you-know-when-a-teaching-strategy-is-most-effective-john-hattie-has-an-idea

Sherman, D., Lokhande, M., Müller, T., & Cohen, G. L. (2021). Self-Affirmation Interventions. In G. M. Walton & A. Crum (Eds.), *Handbook of wise interventions: How social psychology can help people change* (pp. 63–98). The Guilford Press.

Slavin, R. (2018, June 21). John Hattie is wrong. *Robert Slavin's Blog*. https://robertslavinsblog.wordpress.com/2018/06/21/john-hattie-is-wrong/

Sparks, S. D. (2015, March 31). "Middle" students find success tutoring peers, in N.Y.C. study. *Education Week*. www.edweek.org/teaching-learning/middle-students-find-success-tutoring-peers-in-n-y-c-study/2015/03

Sparks, S. D. (2018, August 7). The "brain" in growth mindset: Does teaching students neuroscience help? *Education Week*. www.edweek.org/leadership/the-brain-in-growth-mindset-does-teaching-students-neuroscience-help/2018/08

Stock, E. (2019, January 24). Want students to remember what they learn? Have them teach it. *EdSurge*. www.edsurge.com/news/2019-01-24-want-students-to-remember-what-they-learn-have-them-teach-it

Stone, M. (2014, Spring). *What does it mean to provide cultural support for students?* NMTESOL, Central New Mexico Community College. https://nmtesol.files.wordpress.com/2014/05/nmtesol-spring-2014-stone.pdf

Strauss, V. (2014, March 8). The manipulation of social emotional learning. *The Washington Post*. www.washingtonpost.com/news/answer-sheet/wp/2014/03/08/the-manipulation-of-social-emotional-learning/

Terada, Y. (2021, October 15). The necessity of finding more ways to praise. *Edutopia*. www.edutopia.org/article/necessity-finding-more-ways-praise

Tomlinson, C. A., & Sousa, D. A. (2020). The sciences of teaching. *Education Leadership*, *77*(8). www.ascd.org/el/articles/the-sciences-of-teaching

Tugend, A. (2013, April 6). You've been doing a fantastic job. Just one thing . . . *The New York Times*, 5.

Uchida, A., Michael, R. B., & Mori, K. (2018). An induced successful performance enhances student self-efficacy and boosts academic achievement. *AERA Open*, *4*(4), 233285841880619. https://doi.org/10.1177/2332858418806198

Washburn, K. (2017). Is your school a safe place to fail? *Christian School Education*, *21*(2).

White, J. B., Langer, E. J., Yariv, L., & Welch, J. C. (2006). Frequent social comparisons and destructive emotions and behaviors: The dark side of social comparisons. *Journal of Adult Development*, *13*(1), 36–44. https://doi.org/10.1007/s10804-006-9005-0

Wolff, F., Wigfield, A., Möller, J., Dicke, A.-L., & Eccles, J. S. (2020). Social, dimensional, and temporal comparisons by students and parents: An investigation of the 2I/E model at the transition from elementary to junior high school. *Journal of Educational Psychology*, *112*(8), 1644–1660. https://doi.org/10.1037/edu0000440

Wood, D., Bruner, J. S., & Ross, G. (1976). The role of tutoring in problem solving. *Journal of Child Psychology and Psychiatry*, *17*(2), 89–100. https://doi.org/10.1111/j.1469-7610.1976.tb00381.x

Yeager, D. S., Hanselman, P., Walton, G. M., Murray, J. S., Crosnoe, R., Muller, C., Tipton, E., Schneider, B., Hulleman, C. S., Hinojosa, C. P., Paunesku, D., Romero, C., Flint, K., Roberts, A., Trott, J., Iachan, R., Buontempo, J., Yang, S. M., Carvalho, C. M., . . . Dweck, C. S. (2019). A national experiment reveals where a growth mindset improves achievement. *Nature*, *573*(7774), 364–369. https://doi.org/10.1038/s41586-019-1466-y

Yeager, D. S., Purdie-Vaughns, V., Garcia, J., Apfel, N., Brzustoski, P., Master, A., Hessert, W. T., Williams, M. E., & Cohen, G. L. (2014). Breaking the cycle of mistrust: Wise interventions to provide critical feedback across the racial divide. *Journal of Experimental Psychology: General, 143*(2), 804–824. https://doi.org/10.1037/aoo 33906

Yeager, D. S., Walton, G., & Cohen, G. (2013). Addressing achievement gaps with psychological interventions. *Kappan Magainze, 94*(5), 62–65.

4 What Is "Relatedness" and Why Is it Important?

Researchers describe relatedness as "feeling connected to others, to caring for and being cared for by those others, to having a sense of belongingness both with other individuals and with one's community" (Ryan & Deci, 2000, p. 7). In other words, and in the school context, do students feel comfortable with the quality of their *relationships* in class and at school, does their class work create situations where they connect with others with whom they want to *connect*, and do they feel like they *belong* to some kind of *community*?

Vast quantities of research document the connection between a sense of relatedness at school and intrinsic motivation and academic achievement (Furrer & Skinner, 2003; Xie et al., 2022).

When relatedness is discussed in education contexts, it is often done in these categories (Furrer & Skinner, 2003; Gempp & González-Carrasco, 2021):

- Teacher-to-student
- Student-to-student (peer-to-peer)
- Student-to-class
- Student-to-school (in its entirety)
- Student-to-parent/guardian.

DOI: 10.4324/9781315208824-4

What Is "Relatedness" and Why Is it Important?

Since this book is geared towards classroom teachers, and a single teacher has limited influence on an entire school and minimal influence on a student's parent, this chapter will focus on discussing the first three categories.

Teacher-to-Student

Researchers have found that high-quality teacher-to-student relationships are critical for developing the conditions for intrinsic motivation to grow and for academic success (Sparks, 2019). In fact, studies have found that these kind of positive relationships outweigh subject knowledge as an influence on student achievement (Klassen, 2016). Students "liking" their teacher (Montalvo et al., 2007) is important, bringing research "heft" to what is probably the most-quoted line from the late teacher Rita Pierson's wildly popular TED-Talk (over 14 million views): "Kids don't learn from people they don't like" (Pierson, 2013).

Other elements critical to a positive teacher–student relationship include feeling that their teacher is empathetic to their concerns and experiences (University of Eastern Finland, 2015), is respectful and kind, and demonstrates interest in what is going on in their lives (Greater Good Science Center, 2022).

When teachers consider the kind of relationship they want to develop with their students, it might be worth considering the types that researcher Victoria Theisen-Home (2021) found were prioritized in different teacher education programs. Some trained their student teachers in an "instrumental" focus suggesting that educators identify information and interests as a means to enforce compliance. Others emphasized a "reciprocal" focus that highlighted cooperating together to solve problems (Pietrafetta, n.d.).

This dichotomy is reflective of other similar characterizations describing teacher–student and parent-child relationships, including "transactional" vs. "transformative" (Ferlazzo, 2011a) and "authoritarian" vs. "authoritative" (Ferlazzo, 2015).

Of course, we teachers are the ones ultimately "in charge" of our classrooms, and we want students to do what we ask them to do! But by demonstrating listening skills and the qualities of empathy, respect, and kindness, we are more likely to gain cooperation instead of compliance; our students are more likely to be intrinsically motivated than having to be "pushed along"; and we both are more likely to grow in many ways than we may not have expected. In addition, researchers have found that positive teacher–student relationships can reduce teacher "emotional exhaustion" (Cui, 2022) and "burnout" (Corbin et al., 2019).

Having positive teacher–student relationships does not mean we are *friends*. Instead, we are in a public adult/child relationship where we can be *friendly* (Ferlazzo, 2011b). And concerned. And supportive. And "go the extra mile."

"Establish, Maintain, and Restore" is the name of a framework for developing positive teacher–student relationships. It was developed by Clayton Cook (2018a, 2018b), a professor at the University of Minnesota, in 2018. Its three phases are relatively self-explanatory on the surface—how teachers get to know students initially, how they continue to reinforce those relationships during the year, and how they handle problems that develop in those relationships.

Of course, many good teachers have been thinking through—and acting on—these phases for as long as schools have existed. The strategies listed in this chapter and throughout the book reflect this kind of thinking and planning and were being implemented by me and others long before "Establish, Maintain, and Restore" was unveiled.

Nevertheless, "Establish, Maintain, and Restore" is a clear, concise and easy to remember name for an effective teacher "mindset" about teacher–student relationships. Many effective strategies can fit under its umbrella, and high-quality research supporting it has been developed fairly quickly (Cook et al., 2018a; Duong et al., 2019; Kincade et al., 2020). This kind of evidence, perhaps, can be used to break-through to educators who subscribe to the "Don't Smile Until Christmas" relationship-building belief. It's also an excellent way to frame professional development, and a "graspable" concept for teacher education programs.

And it's definitely a good lens to use when reading this chapter.

EDTECH TOOLBOX

For more information about "Establish, Maintain, and Restore," visit "The Best Resources for Learning about the 'Establish-Maintain-Restore' Classroom Management Approach" (https://larry ferlazzo.edublogs.org/2022/08/01/the-best-re sources-for-learning-about-the-establish-main tain-restore-classroom-management-approach/). You can find many other good ideas there for ways to develop and solidify positive teacher–student relationships.

Student-to-Student (Peer-to-Peer)

Having supportive peer relationships, especially for adolescents (Greater Good Science Center, 2022), has been found to positively impact student intrinsic motivation and academic achievement (Holden, 2002; Mikami et al., 2017; Wentzel, 1998). Research in the workplace, which may very well be applicable to school environments, finds that people are more energized, creative, and productive when trust among coworkers is high (Ferlazzo, 2018).

Student-to-Class

Student-to-class relatedness is connected to a sense of belonging—do students feel like they are part of a community (OECD, 2017). Though many analyses of this kind of connectedness focus on a school-wide perspective, in both class and overall school-wide settings teacher and peer relationships make huge contributions towards students feeling this general sense of belongingness (Henchy et al., 2009). And this sense of belonging, in turn, influences the development of motivation and academic success (Xie et al., 2022).

In addition to surveying students' feelings about their relationships with teachers and peers, some of the other factors researchers measure to evaluate students' sense of belonging in classes and in schools include: if they feel like outsiders in their class (Zhao et al., 2019); how much they feel like they matter to others (Panorama Education, n.d.); do they feel like a "real part" of the class or school (Knekta et al., 2020); and/or simply do they feel like they "belong" (Barr & Gibson, 2013).

What Are Ways Teachers Can Support Students' Sense of Relatedness?

Many of the strategies listed in other chapters have been found to support building students' sense of relatedness. Here are even more—the ones listed first more specifically relate to developing positive teacher–student relationships, while the later ones have more relevance to enhancing peer-to-peer relationships and developing a sense of class community.

32. Saying Students' Names Correctly and Greeting Them by Name

If we teachers want to have a positive relationship with our students, we need to make pronouncing student names correctly a priority. As former New York City Schools Chancellor Carmen Fariña has said, based on her own experience as a child, "Mispronouncing a student's name essentially renders that student invisible" (Mitchell, 2016). Research backs up her contention and shows that mispronouncing a student's name can have negative social and emotional consequences (Chhabra Rice, 2017). And that research, in turn, is reinforced by informal surveys of my own students (Ferlazzo, 2016) and, I suspect, by similar surveys if they were done by many other teachers.

If I'm unsure how to pronounce a student's name, on the first day of school I will ask them how to say it correctly before I try to say it. I'll then try again and ask if I am saying it correctly. If I am, I'll write down how to say it phonetically. Oftentimes, a student will say something like, "It's okay, you can just call me (some "easier"-to-pronounce name)." My immediate response is always, "You have the right to be called your name, and I will do that. Unless, of course, you prefer to be called something else" (I actually make that point with all students, including those whose names I can easily pronounce—I'll call them whatever they want, and that includes their choice of pronouns). Almost always, students respond by saying they would like to be called their actual name.

I keep the phonetic list on my desk and, at first, review it before each class period. I'm usually able to do a pretty good job, though I might make a couple of stumbles at first. I always have a large supply of healthful packaged fruit snacks in my room, and after the first week-and-a-half of the school year I have a policy of giving one to any student whose name I don't remember or whose name I mispronounce. The potential treats turn my remembering student names into a fun game for everyone that "keeps me on my toes" as students are always asking me "What's my name?" or "How do you say my name?" during the first month. It's the only time my students "want" me to not remember their name or mispronounce it!

In addition to saying and remembering names, greeting students by name each day is equally important. Studies have shown that greeting students at the door has a positive impact on the teacher–student relationship, along with other benefits (Cook et al., 2018b). However, researchers have not compared that kind of welcoming with other specific greetings. I prefer to be in my classroom as students enter and greet them individually by name and help them be focused on what they need to do and see them doing it. That last part is difficult to do if I'm greeting students at the door. Because of the way the research was structured, it is not clear if it was the greeting at the door or the actual greeting that made the difference. Based on my personal experience, it's the latter that is most important.

Studies have found that hearing your name said elicits a strong reaction from your brain (Carmody & Lewis, 2006), so strong, in fact, that the brain of a person in a vegetative state reacts in a similar way when they hear their name (Staffen et al., 2006). It doesn't seem clear what that reaction means, but it's certainly a strong reaction, and not a negative one (NameCoach, 2017).

If we don't say all of our students' names, then it's possible, if not probable, that some of them may not hear their name said by anyone during the course of a day—and experience that strong neuro response. They all deserve to be "named."

EDTECH TOOLBOX

For more information about the impact mispronouncing names can have on our students, and for advice on learning on to pronounce them correctly, visit "The Best Resources on the Importance of Correctly Pronouncing Student Names" (https://larryferlazzo.edublogs.org/2016/06/11/the-best-resources-on-the-importance-of-correctly-pronouncing-student-names/).

33. Exchanging Letters

At the beginning of each school year, I share with students a letter I've addressed to them. You can see an example of one in Figure 4.1. I show it on the document camera and also read it aloud as an introduction to me. It also serves as a model for a letter I invite them to write to me (I ask them questions in my letter), though I also explain that they don't necessarily have to produce a letter—they could also create a poster containing the same information. The letter I write for my English Language Learner Newcomers class is obviously very different from the one in the Figure, and yours can be adjusted for its audience, too.

Their return letter provides important information for me to know and, as a side benefit, it can also be a good writing formative assessment. But its true benefit is in what comes next.

The night I collect the students' letters I sit down with them and some pads of medium size sticky notes (depending on the number of students I have that year, sometimes I review them over two or even three nights). I scribble a short comment and question for each student on one of the notes and put it on their letter.

To a student who says they like to play baseball, I might write: "I played second base when I was in Little League. What position do you play and what's the hardest part of playing it?"

To one who writes that they like to watch a lot of Netflix, I might write: "My favorite Netflix show is 'Stranger Things.' What's your favorite and why do you like it so much?"

I then return the letters the following day or shortly thereafter, explaining that I appreciated learning about each of them. I ask them to take a minute and read what I wrote on the sticky note, and write a response. It's not unusual for students to comment that they are surprised that I read their letters, much less responded to them.

I'll then recollect the letters and glance through them. But the message has been heard—at least by most: "Mr. Ferlazzo actually reads our stuff and takes it seriously. Maybe he takes *us* seriously."

Dear Students,

Welcome back to school! I'm excited and nervous. I love teaching, and getting to know students each year, though I will miss a summer of staying up late and being able to sleep in.

I've been teaching here at Burbank for over twenty years, and love a lot of things about it: the teachers are very caring, the students work hard and are also very kind, and the principal and assistant principals really try to support both teachers and students. Some things I don't like about the school include the buildings are a bit old and many of our rooms only have one electrical outlet, sometimes the heating and air conditioning don't work that well, and during a big rainstorm our roof leaks sometimes. What do you like about school? It doesn't have to be about Burbank—it can be about school in general. What don't you like about school?

My family is important to me. I've been married for many years and have three children and four grandchildren. My wife is a retired nurse practitioner—sort of between a nurse and a doctor. One daughter works in a company helping to hire people, another daughter is a hair stylist, and our son is in the military. Two of our granddaughters are babies—one is still bald like me and a friend told me we look like we have "come from the same planet." Our other two grandchildren are older and in college. What is your family like?

Three things that you might want to know about me are: One, I was born without a sense of smell and have never smelled anything in my

Figure 4.1   Teacher letter example.

whole life. Not having a sense of smell limits my sense of taste, and I can only taste things that are very "strong." That's why I put lots of hot sauce on many things I eat. Two, I love to play Pickleball and basketball, and have a decent three-point shot, though my teammates might not agree with me. And, three, I speak Spanish, and studied in Mexico and Guatemala. What are three things you would like me to know about you? What do you like to do when you are not in school?

I am looking forward to spending the school year with you. We'll get to know each other and learn from our successes and our mistakes— I make a lot of them! And we should have some fun doing it all together!

Sincerely,
Mr. Ferlazzo

Figure 4.1 Continued

34. Weekly Online "Check-Ins"

Verbally checking in with each student every week to see how they are doing is an aspirational goal. However, especially for secondary teachers, it's challenging to find the time to do it, and there's no guarantee that students are going to be in the mood to share candid responses. I have found that asking students to complete a very short Google Form each week has been an important tool for building positive relationships with students, but only because I verbally follow-up with them based on what they write! As mentioned in Chapter 2, the only thing worse than not giving a Check-In survey is giving one and not paying any attention to the responses. If that's the case, it's a safe bet that teacher–student relationships will worsen, not improve.

It's important to keep the number of questions quite low—I keep mine to six, though Panorama Education, an international company specializing in student surveys, recommends five as the maximum (Buckle, n.d.).

Every Monday morning, my students have a few minutes in class to answer these questions (I might add or subtract one depending on the time of year, what is happening in our classes, or what is happening in the world). Some require an answer using a one-to-five linear scale, while others need a short narrative:

1. How are you feeling about our class right now?
2. How are you feeling about school in general?
3. How are you feeling today about things in your personal life?
4. What is one goal you would like to accomplish this school week?
5. Please try to remember the goal you wrote down for last week. Did you accomplish it? Just click yes

or no. But also take a few minutes to think: If you did accomplish it, what did you do that helped you be successful? If you did not accomplish it, what could you have done differently?

6. Is there anything else you think it would be helpful for me to know about how you or your family are doing?

(Ferlazzo & Hull-Sypnieski, 2022, p. 409)

Initially, like with the letter activity, many students are shocked when I follow-up with them on their responses—they assume I wouldn't even look at it. The next day, I always make a point of talking with students who have rated themselves a two or below on any of the linear scale questions, or if they have written other concerning information. Then, in subsequent days, I take a quick look at the survey results prior to each class and am able to make individual comments to other students. I obviously don't respond to everyone, but I do it enough for students to know that I take what they write seriously.

35. Being Conscious of "Teacher Talk"

What we say in the classroom and how we say it, also known as "teacher talk," can have a major impact on the quality of teacher–student relationships. Teachers sharing their personal stories (students love hearing about my dog!), having a light-hearted and joking attitude sometimes, being positive and starting every day "fresh" are some of the things students have told researchers they value most (Sethi & Scales, 2020).

In my experience, I have also found that five words in particular have had a huge impact on my relationships with students: "Thank you," "Please," and "I'm sorry." It's important to note that saying these words sincerely is what makes the difference—I suspect we have all both said them and had them said to us in a sarcastic tone. Using these words often "costs" us nothing, and lets us be good models of behavior in the process.

There are many, many "guides" out there about the "right" way to apologize. If I make a "logistical" mistake about due dates or what page we're on in the textbook, a quick "I'm sorry" will do. If I have made a larger mistake where I have actually caused harm to someone (perhaps by mistakenly accusing them of doing something or inappropriately letting my temper get the best of me and not being as respectful as I should have been), it's a different story. In those kinds of cases, I've made my own modifications to some of those guides (Heaney, 2017). I will follow my "I'm sorry" with an explanation, though not a justification ("I was very tired and was not thinking clearly"); then accepting responsibility ("I know better"). If my mistake was a public one, I make the apology in public; if it was a mistake I made in private, then I'll just say it to the individual student.

EDTECH TOOLBOX

There are many other ways we teachers can strengthen our bonds with students or weaken them through what we say, and you can learn about them at "The Best Resources Sharing Recommendations About 'Teacher Talk'" (https:// larryferlazzo.edublogs.org/2021/06/29/the-best-resources-sharing-recommendations-about-teacher-talk/).

36. Classroom Rituals

There are more definitions of the word "ritual" out there than you can shake a stick at. One, suggested by Mason Currey, an author of a book on rituals, defines them as regular activities that move people into a different kind of "mental or emotional" mindset (Nguyen, 2022). In other words, doing them helps you become more focused. Others define it as a tool to connect to a broader community—in the case of education, the school or class (Mullis & Fincher, 1996). It seems to me that combining both of these definitions works best to help teachers think about what rituals are and how they can fit into our classroom culture and help our students develop their sense of relatedness.

Some of the strategies discussed in previous chapters, such as Class Leadership Team meetings and students regularly sharing about good things that have happened to them during the week or things they are grateful for, can fit into this combined definition for a ritual. The next two strategies—"Daily Dedications" and "Connection or Community Building Circles"— are also clearly rituals.

Thinking about rituals in the classroom can be another opportunity to view our students through the lens of "assets" and not "deficits." After briefly explaining what rituals are, their purposes, and their importance, inviting students to share the rituals they use in their lives can be a bonding classroom experience. Taking the discussion a step further, teachers can invite students to share their own ideas for new rituals that the class can experiment with together. For example, based on a student's suggestion one year, we began to start each class that followed lunch with one minute of lights out and soft music. It helped calm the class down so much that we continued doing it for the rest of the year!

37. Daily Dedications

"Daily Dedications" is an idea borrowed and slightly modified from teacher Harry Seton (2021). The idea is that students take turns presenting a figure who inspires them and to whom they want to dedicate that day of learning. After seeing my example in Figure 4.2, students read these directions and prepare a slide to present on a shared Google Slideshow:

> Choose a date and put your name on it. You can make your slide look anyway you want.
>
> Pick a real or fictional character who inspires you, and explain why and how he/she inspires you. It can be a family member, someone who's famous, a movie character, someone you read about in a book or online. You only have to write three-or-four sentences, and insert an image.
>
> One student will dedicate each class to their inspiration. This is a way to celebrate our classroom community, recognize that our learning is a serious effort that can and should be inspiring, and, hopefully, move all of us to do our best.

This ritual seems to strengthen relationships and a sense of class community as we all begin to learn a little bit about each other's stories, as well as providing a space to focus at the beginning of class. In addition, since many students choose family members as their source of inspiration, it's an opportunity to strengthen those bonds, as well—I can't count how many times students have told me their parents, grandparents, or siblings cried after they showed their slides to them!

I generally do a class "round" of these dedications one time each semester. I generally offer an option of follow-up presentations where students show a baby picture of themselves, along with a story about them from their infant years they learn from family members. Most classes choose to do it and, though the frame of mind those presentations lead to might not accurately be described as "focused" (abundant laughter is what we all generally spend our time doing), it does definitely seem to build class bonds.

What Is "Relatedness" and Why Is it Important?

I'd like to dedicate my teaching and learning today to my father. He was an immigrant from Italy and became a college teacher. Though he left that position to work in business, he continued to teach English to new immigrants at night. He was kind to all and was a good man. He inspired me to want to leave the world a better place than it was when I entered it.

Mr. Ferlazzo

Figure 4.2   Daily dedication teacher example.

38. Connection or Community-Building Circles

Connection Circles, also called Community Building Circles or Proactive Community Circle, are a subset of Restorative Practices, which is a broader field designed to move schools and other institutions away from punitive disciplinary procedures. I support this broader effort. However, many schools have discovered that applying it as a conflict resolution strategy takes expertise and training (Wang & Lee, 2019) that not all teachers may have or be in a position to obtain.

The vast majority of teachers, though, presently have the skills now to periodically use Connection Circles as a way to build community, and research has shown they can successfully achieve that goal. They can also be used as a way to help students begin to constructively process emotions in the face of an immediate traumatic current event (July 6th Insurrection, the murder of George Floyd). One of the reasons they are also called Proactive Community Circles is because they are designed to strengthen relationships as a way to stop conflicts before they occur (Lenertz, 2018).

Here is an outline of the steps involved in a Connection Circle (there are variations—see the EdTech Tool Box for additional resources):

1. The first step is to organize students into a . . . circle. This structure conveys the message that everyone is to be respected and treated equally.
2. The teacher welcomes the group and, perhaps, shares a quotation to help the group get focused. There may be times when well-prepared students can take this role.
3. The teacher introduces the "talking piece" and explains its significance to them. A talking piece is to be passed around the circle, and only the person holding it may speak (though the teacher

retains the right to help clarify, ask a question, or move things along). Students are asked to speak honestly and to "say just enough"—it's important for people not to feel rushed, but it's also important for everyone to get a chance to speak.

4. Teachers also highlight the need for privacy— "what is said in the circle stays in the circle." However, during the first class Connection Circle, it would be important for teachers to point out that they are "mandated reporters" and must report if any student seems to be in danger. Students can also be reminded that there are other school and non-school resources available to provide support, and that students can speak with the teacher privately later.

5. The teacher introduces the guiding question. You can find many ideas for these by searching online for "Connection Circle Questions," as well as visiting the resource in the EdTech Tool Box. The International Institute for Restorative Practices offers four suggested categories (IIRP, 2021):

- Getting Acquainted (Can you share a happy childhood memory? Please describe your favorite meal.)
- Exploring Values (What change would you like to see in the community? What demonstrates respect?)
- Storytelling (Share a time when you were outside your comfort zone)
- Relating to the Curriculum (What is the best and worst thing about this science project?)

If the purpose of the circle is to respond to a current event, the question could be "How are you feeling about _____ and what questions, if any, do you have about it?)

6. The "talking piece" is then passed around. No one is required to speak. If they pass, they can ask for it to be given back to them if they change their mind at some point.

7. After everyone has spoken, the teacher may or may not make brief concluding comments. Then there's a closing "ceremony," which could be something like everyone turning to the person next to them and telling them thanks for participating, or a "class chant."

I tend to use these circles to discuss more substantial questions than the ones used in some of the "lighter" activities listed under Community Building Activities" later in this chapter.

These kinds of circles can be very valuable and take time if you have a large class. I generally do this activity about once every month.

EDTECH TOOLBOX

For more information about Restorative Practices, including more advice on organizing Connection Circles, visit "The Best Resources for Learning about Restorative Practices—Help Me Find More" (https://larryferlazzo.edublogs.org/2015/05/02/the-best-resources-for-learning-about-restorative-practices-help-me-find-more/).

39. Cooperative Learning

Various types of cooperative learning have been discussed in previous chapters, including Project-Based Learning, Problem-Based Learning, and

What Is "Relatedness" and Why Is it Important?

Jigsaws. In addition to motivational and academic benefits that group work brings to students' sense of autonomy and competence, research shows it also enhances peer-to-peer relatedness (Van Ryzin, Roseth, & Biglan, 2020; Van Ryzin & Roseth, 2019). Some studies have shown that students of color particularly gain these benefits (Van Ryzin, Roseth, & McClure, 2020).

EDTECH TOOLBOX

Visit "The Best Sites for Cooperative & Collaborative Learning Ideas" (https://larryfer lazzo.edublogs.org/2010/04/02/the-best-sites-for-cooperative-learning-ideas/ for even more ideas on how to implement this strategy in your classroom).

40. Community-Building Activities

Building a sense of community in the classroom begins by "helping students know and care about each other" (Cheney, 2002).

Here are a few simple community building activities that I regularly use.

Adding a Community Building Question to Group Activities

A simple community-building strategy I use throughout the year is when I am dividing students into "think-write-pair-share" groups, I often will have them answer a personal question in addition to the focused academic one. These questions might be

140

ones like "What is your favorite ice-cream?"; "If you could have a superpower, which one would it be?" or a request like "Please show your partner a picture you took on your phone that you like." Sometimes, it's a simple "Would You Rather . . ." question (search online for countless lists of these questions appropriate for class). To ensure that they don't use all their group time on the personal question, I will usually ask students to just spend a short time on it and will publicly say when that time is up. When the class reconvenes, I typically ask one-or-two students to share their personal response before getting to the academic task. See the EdTech Box for links to good lists of these kinds of "ice-breaker" prompts.

Two Truths and a Lie

The Two Truths and a Lie game is always a winner. Near the beginning of the year, I have students write down their name and two truths and one lie about themselves on a slide in a shared Google Slides presentation. Every day for two-or-three weeks two-or-three students present their slide at the beginning or end of class, and the class votes on which one is the lie.

"Appreciation, Apology, Aha!"

I learned about the "Appreciation, Apology, Aha!" strategy from teacher Aukeem Ballard via an Edutopia video (Edutopia, 2018). Regularly during the year, though not every day, near the end of class I ask students to write down either an *Appreciation* (Who would they like to compliment and why?); an *Apology* (Who might they have caused harm to in the

141

class and to whom they would like to make amends?) or an *Aha*! (What is something they learned in class that they thought was particularly important or interesting?). In the version I do, I add on *Good News* (even though it ruins the alliteration). Studies have shown that sharing good news, and having it received positively, improves relationships and a sense of community (Barker, 2022). This "good news" can be from any part of the student's life. Everyone then gets out of their seats and stands next to one of the classroom walls—an imperfect circle. I then call on volunteers to share, and also choose others. Everyone is prepared (or should be!) because they have already written a response, and everyone's comments are responded to by brief applause.

Time Traveler Activity

A quick community-building "lesson" I do a few times during the year is what teacher Valentina Melnikova (2022) calls a "Time Traveler Activity." There are websites that allow you to find new words that were added to dictionaries on the year you were born, important history events that took place on the day you were born, as well as what was the top song on your birthday, and even what the NASA Hubble Space Telescope saw on that day. Having students choose a word or an event, or share a song or image and, most importantly, share their reasons for choosing it or their impressions of it, provide another opportunity for students to get to know each other, including their interests, what things might be important or interesting to them and, of course, the date of their birthday! As Valentina points out, though, it's probably a good idea for the teacher to double-check the words added to the dictionary in the year or years your students were most likely born just to make sure they are all classroom appropriate. It's probably less of a concern with the number one song since it's likely your school district's Internet Content filter will have blocked it if it wasn't appropriate. See the EdTech Tool Box for a list of sites your students can use for this activity.

Potlucks

Researchers have found that sharing a meal together enhances the creation of social bonds, and an occasional class potluck is one way to apply that finding in the classroom. Yes, we need to be aware of food allergies; yes, it's probably best to have it outside because of the COVID epidemic; and, yes, we teachers need tell students if they can't contribute because of financial or living-arrangement issues they should talk to us privately and we'll pick up something for them. But even with these challenges, I think having a potluck once or twice during the school year is worth the effort.

Human Scavenger Hunts and Facing History

Other community building activities that I use in the beginning of the year are "Find Someone in the Class Who . . ." Scavenger Hunts (see the EdTech Tool Box for resources) and Facing History & Ourselves' (Facing History & Ourselves, 2022) collection of back to school resources.

Friday Reflections

One last activity I use quasi-regularly during the year is to have students do a Friday reflection. Sometimes students write about what went well that week or something they are grateful for (see Chapter 3). Other times it's a response to the question "What made your week?" (Glazer, 2022) or asking how they are feeling about a particular situation that recently arose. Afterwards, students share what they wrote with partners and some tell the entire class.

EDTECH TOOLBOX

You can find tons of ideas for "icebreaker" prompts to use with students at "The Best Lists Of 'Icebreaker' Prompts—Please Share Your Own" (https://larryferlazzo.edublogs.org/2022/07/31/the-best-lists-of-icebreaker-prompts-please-share-your-own/).

Sites that will tell your students about what happened on their birthday or the year of their birth can be found at "The Best Sites Where You Can Find Cool Things That Happened On Your Birthday" (https://larryferlazzo.edublogs.org/2020/04/02/the-best-sites-where-you-can-find-cool-things-that-happened-on-your-birthday/) and at "The Best 'Today In History' Sites" (https://larryferlazzo.edublogs.org/2008/06/11/the-best-today-in-history-sites/).

Find several lesson plans, and examples, of student Identity Self-Portraits at "Three Excellent Student Identity 'Self-Portrait' Activities" (https://larryferlazzo.edublogs.org/2022/07/30/three-excellent-student-identity-self-portrait-activities/). "'Human Scavenger Hunt' Worksheets To Help Begin The Year" (https://

larryferlazzo.edublogs.org/2022/07/31/human-scavenger-hunt-worksheets-to-help-begin-the-year/) has links to "find someone in the class who . . ." resources, which can also be used in bingo card form.

41. Supporting Students' Identities

By acknowledging and celebrating identities that students "claim" as their own, in contrast to identities that might be "assigned" to them by others (https://edukitchen.net/student-identity-in-the-online-class room/), teachers can help develop environments where students feel safe to be "who they are" with their classmates. This security can promote a sense of belongingness, which was highlighted earlier in this chapter as being a critical prerequisite for encouraging intrinsic motivation.

Here are two simple activities that can be small, but important, steps towards helping students begin to feel safe in the classroom.

Identity Self-Portraits

These are good activities to help students reflect on who they are, and for them to learn about the diversity in their classroom. You can find links to several different lesson plans, and examples, in the EdTech Toolbox. One of them is from Shana V. White, who has students draw an outline of themselves, and then put a line down the middle. On the left side, they draw what they physically look like. On the right side,

What Is "Relatedness" and Why Is it Important?

they draw and label parts of their identity that people would not necessarily know by looking at them (what they like to do, goals, etc.) (www.edutopia.org/article/creating-learning-environment-where-all-kids-feel-valued).

"I Am" Posters and Presentations

At the beginning of the year, students complete an "I Am" poster by completing these sentences (I do one as a model):

I love _____ because _____
    I wonder _____
    I am happy when _____
    I am scared when _____
    I worry about _____ because _____
    I hope to _____
    I am sad when _____
    In the future, I will _____
            (Ferlazzo & Hull-Sypnieski, 2022, p. 28)

Students present the posters to each other through a "speed-dating" style where they are seated in rows, and alternate rows move to the next desk after every few minutes. Then, to ensure that at least most students in class learn about each other, I put students who were in the same "row" into groups of three and then present their posters again. Those letter groups of three present to each other and then work together to create a three-circle Venn Diagram representing what they said on their posters. If I'm even more ambitious, I have them next ask each other questions to see what other commonalities/differences they can find to add to the diagram.

EDTECH TOOLBOX

Multiple ideas and lesson plans for student identity activities can be found at "Three Excellent Student Identity 'Self-Portrait' Activities" (https://larryferlazzo.edublogs.org/2022/07/30/three-excellent-student-identity-self-portrait-activities/).

What Questions Can Teachers Ask Themselves to Ensure Their Strategies to Promote Student Relatedness Are Also Culturally Responsive?

- Researchers have found that white teachers generally have weaker relationships with students of color (Cherng, 2017). Is that the case with me? What would students of color in my classes say about their relationship with me? What can I do to strengthen those relationships?

- Some studies suggest that teachers and schools that have "colorblindness" policies where diversity and differences are not recognized and acknowledged leads to reduced levels of academic achievement for students of color (Celeste et al., 2019). Am I serious about applying Culturally Responsive Teaching strategies to help ensure that this doesn't happen to students of color in my classes? Or am I just interested in applying CRT in a "performative" manner?

- When asking students about their families, am I open to, and supportive of, family units that might be different from what some might consider the "typical American family"?

- Do I communicate to some students that their name is a difficult one to pronounce and, in effect, send a message that there is something wrong with them? Or, do I send a message that they've got a great name, I'm sorry I'm having difficulty saying it correctly, and that I want to say it correctly, I will say it correctly and that it is my responsibility to do so? In other words, do I, instead, communicate that the difficulty is with me?

- Am I showing any implicit or explicit prejudice when and how I talk with students? For example, when I hear some kind of disruption in class, do I immediately turn to some students who might be from the same race or culture? Might I, implicitly or explicitly, be communicating to the class that I believe certain groups of the same race or culture are more likely to be disruptive than others? If I send "referrals" to the office, are there patterns to them that might indicate implicit or explicit bias?

- Would my students describe me as someone who looks at them as "just students in my class" or would they describe me as someone who is interested in their lives, their cultures, their challenges, and their goals? What more can I do to be the kind of teacher fitting the second description?

- Am I creating time and space in my classroom for discussions about potentially "uncomfortable" conversations related to what might be happening in the world at the moment, about race, and about culture? Or, am I unwilling to venture beyond light topics and am I just simply "covering the curriculum"?

- Do I regularly look for ways to help develop students' leadership skills? For example, do I sometimes prepare students to lead activities like the "Appreciation, Apology, Aha!" activities or even

Connection Circles? When I do this kind of leadership development, do I ensure that I'm doing so with a diverse group of students?

- How do I respond if and when a student makes a racist, sexist, homophobic or transphobic comment? Do I pretend to not have heard it? Do I challenge them and then look for ways to structure positive conversations about race, gender and LGBTQ+ issues in our society?
- Are the only times I create opportunities to highlight students' racial and cultural identities when we do Identity Self Portraits and, perhaps, during times in the year when I'm "supposed to" (Black History Month, Martin Luther King, Jr. Day, Hispanic Heritage Month, etc.). Or do I make this a year-round practice?
- Am I aware of, and do I respect, the significance and importance of religious and non-religious holidays recognized in my students' cultures that are different from the ones I appreciate in my own life?

References

Barker, E. (2022). What's an easy way to strengthen your relationships? *Barking Up the Wrong Tree*. https://bakadesuyo.com/2010/08/whats-an-easy-way-to-strengthen-your-relation/

Barr, R. D., & Gibson, E. L. (2013). *Building a culture of hope: Enriching schools with optimism and opportunity.* Solution Tree Press.

Buckle, J. (n.d.). 21 quick questions to check in on your students' well-being in 2022–23. *Panorama Education.* www.panoramaed.com/blog/21-questions-check-in-student-sel-wellbeing

Carmody, D. P., & Lewis, M. (2006). Brain activation when hearing one's own and others' names. *Brain Research*, *1116*(1), 153–158. https://doi.org/10.1016/j.brainres.2006.07.121

Celeste, L., Baysu, G., Phalet, K., Meeussen, L., & Kende, J. (2019). Can school diversity policies reduce belonging and achievement gaps between minority and majority youth? Multiculturalism, colorblindness, and assimilationism assessed. *Personality and Social Psychology Bulletin, 45*(11), 1603–1618. https://doi.org/10.1177/0146167219838577

Cheney, M. (2002). "Community in the classroom: a research synthesis". ScholarWorks at University of Montana. Graduate Student Theses, Dissertations, & Professional Papers. 7916. https://scholarworks.umt.edu/cgi/viewcontent.cgi?article=8951&context=etd

Cherng, H.-Y. S. (2017). The ties that bind: Teacher relationships, academic expectations, and racial/ethnic and generational inequality. *American Journal of Education, 124*(1), 67–100. https://doi.org/10.1086/693955

Chhabra Rice, O. (2017, November 15). Pronouncing students' names correctly should be a big deal. *Education Week.* www.edweek.org/leadership/opinion-pronouncing-students-names-correctly-should-be-a-big-deal/2017/11

Cook, C. R., Coco, S., Zhang, Y., Fiat, A. E., Duong, M. T., Renshaw, T. L., Long, A. C., & Frank, S. (2018a). Cultivating positive teacher–student relationships: Preliminary evaluation of the Establish–Maintain–Restore (EMR) method. *School Psychology Review, 47*(3), 226–243. https://doi.org/10.17105/SPR-2017-0025.V47-3

Cook, C. R., Fiat, A., Larson, M., Daikos, C., Slemrod, T., Holland, E. A., Thayer, A. J., & Renshaw, T. (2018b). Positive greetings at the door: Evaluation of a low-cost, high-yield proactive classroom management strategy. *Journal of Positive Behavior Interventions, 20*(3), 149–159. https://doi.org/10.1177/1098300717753831

Corbin, C. M., Alamos, P., Lowenstein, A. E., Downer, J. T., & Brown, J. L. (2019). The role of teacher–student relationships in predicting teachers' personal accomplishment and emotional exhaustion. *Journal of School Psychology, 77*, 1–12. https://doi.org/10.1016/j.jsp.2019.10.001

Cui, L. (2022). The role of teacher–student relationships in predicting teachers' occupational wellbeing, emotional exhaustion, and enthusiasm. *Frontiers in Psychology*, *13*, 896813. https://doi.org/10.3389/fpsyg.2022.896813

Duong, M. T., Pullmann, M. D., Buntain-Ricklefs, J., Lee, K., Benjamin, K. S., Nguyen, L., & Cook, C. R. (2019). Brief teacher training improves student behavior and student–teacher relationships in middle school. *School Psychology*, *34*(2), 212–221. https://doi.org/10.1037/spq0000296

Edutopia (Director). (2018, August 10). 60-second strategy: Appreciation, apology, aha! [Video]. www.youtube.com/watch?v=qIel4r3uK9k&list=PL10g2YT_ln2hGQkIsIJxXMLY7wv6kFIUF&index=22

Facing History & Ourselves. (2022). Activities for the first days of school. www.facinghistory.org/resource-library/back-school-building-community-connection-and-learning/activities-first-days-school

Ferlazzo, L. (2011a, May 25). Being "transactional" versus being "transformational" in schools. *Huffpost*. www.huffpost.com/entry/being-transactional-versu_b_779984

Ferlazzo, L. (2011b, October 25). Response: Can teachers be friends with students? Part one. *Education Week Opinion*. www.edweek.org/teaching-learning/opinion-response-can-teachers-be-friends-with-students-part-one/2011/10

Ferlazzo, L. (2015, June 10). Study: "Authoritative," not "authoritarian," classroom management works best for boys. *Larry Ferlazzo's Website of the Day*. https://larryferlazzo.edublogs.org/2015/06/10/study-authoritative-not-authoritarian-classroom-management-works-best-for-boys/

Ferlazzo, L. (2016, October 23). What my students say about teachers mispronouncing their names. *Larry Ferlazzo's Website of the Day*. https://larryferlazzo.edublogs.org/2016/10/23/what-my-students-say-about-teachers-mispronouncing-their-names/

Ferlazzo, L. (2018, June 6). Study: People are more engaged & creative if they trust the people they are working with . . . *Larry Ferlazzo's Website of the Day*. https://larryferlazzo.edublogs.org/2018/06/06/study-people-are-more-engaged-creative-if-they-trust-the-people-they-are-working-with/

Ferlazzo, L., & Hull-Sypnieski, K. (2022). *The ESL/ELL teacher's survival guide: Ready-to-use strategies, tools,* and activities for teaching English language learners of all levels (2nd edition). Jossey-Bass.

Furrer, C., & Skinner, E. (2003). Sense of relatedness as a factor in children's academic engagement and performance. *Journal of Educational Psychology*, 95(1), 148–162. https://doi.org/10.1037/0022-0663.95.1.148

Gempp, R., & González-Carrasco, M. (2021). Peer relatedness, school satisfaction, and life satisfaction in early adolescence: A non-recursive model. *Frontiers in Psychology*, 12, 641714. https://doi.org/10.3389/fpsyg.2021.641714

Glazer, R. (2022). My team asks each other this 1 question every week, and it changed our culture for the better. *Inc.* www.inc.com/robert-glazer/how-a-surprising-slack-channel-strengthened-our-companys-culture.html

Greater Good Science Center. (2022). Positive teacher–student relationships. *Greater Good in Education.* https://ggie.berkeley.edu/school-relationships/positive-teacher–student-relationships/

Heaney, K. (2017, June 8). The apology critics who want to teach you how to say you're sorry. *The Cut.* www.thecut.com/2017/06/these-apology-critics-want-to-teach-you-how-to-say-sorry.html

Henchy, A., Cunningham, J., & Bradley, K. (2009). Measuring Latino students' perceptions of school belonging: A Rasch measurement application. www.uky.edu/~kdbrad2/Alex.pdf

Holden, A. (2002). The effects of parents, teachers, and peers on academic motivation [masters thesis]. Eastern Illinois University. https://thekeep.eiu.edu/theses/1521/

IIRP. (2021). *Sample prompting questions/topics for circles.* International Institute for Restorative Practices. www.iirp.edu/images/conf_downloads/RZrVvi_Sample_Prompting_Circles_Questions.pdf

Kincade, L., Cook, C., & Goerdt, A. (2020). Meta-analysis and common practice elements of universal approaches to improving student–teacher relationships. *Review of Educational Research*, 90(5), 710–748. https://doi.org/10.3102/0034654320946836

Klassen, R. (2016, March 2). Can you spot a good teacher from their characteristics? *The Guardian.* www.the

guardian.com/teacher-network/2016/mar/02/can-you-spot-a-good-teacher-from-their-characteristics

Knekta, E., Chatzikyriakidou, K., & McCartney, M. (2020). Evaluation of a questionnaire measuring university students' sense of belonging to and involvement in a biology department. *CBE—Life Sciences Education, 19*(3), ar27. https://doi.org/10.1187/cbe.19-09-0166

Lenertz, M. (2018). The impact of proactive community circles on student academic achievement and student behavior in an elementary setting [dissertation] (174). Dissertations. https://digitalcommons.umassglobal.edu/edd_dissertations/174?utm_source=digitalcommons.umassglobal.edu%2Fedd_dissertations%2F174&utm_medium=PDF&utm_campaign=PDFCoverPages

Melnikova, V. (2022, June 23). 6 ways to get to know your students and build a classroom community. *Edutopia.* www.edutopia.org/article/6-ways-get-know-your-students-and-build-classroom-community?utm_content=linkpos2&utm_campaign=weekly-2022–06–29&utm_source=edu-newsletter&utm_medium=email

Mikami, A. Y., Ruzek, E. A., Hafen, C. A., Gregory, A., & Allen, J. P. (2017). Perceptions of relatedness with classroom peers promote adolescents' behavioral engagement and achievement in secondary school. *Journal of Youth and Adolescence, 46*(11), 2341–2354. https://doi.org/10.1007/s10964-017-0724-2

Mitchell, C. (2016, May 16). A teacher mispronouncing a student's name can have a lasting impact. *PBS News Hour.* www.pbs.org/newshour/education/a-teacher-mispronouncing-a-students-name-can-have-a-lasting-impact

Montalvo, G. P., Mansfield, E. A., & Miller, R. B. (2007). Liking or disliking the teacher: Student motivation, engagement and achievement. *Evaluation & Research in Education, 20*(3), 144–158. https://doi.org/10.2167/eri406.0

Mullis, F., & Fincher, S. (1996). Using rituals to define the school community. *Elementary School Guidance & Counseling, 30*(4), 243–251.

NameCoach. (2017, November 12). The brain on your name: How your brain responds to the sound of your name. https://name-coach.com/blog/brain-name-brain-responds-sound-name/

Nguyen, T. (2022, June 15). Why we need rituals, not routines. *Vox.* www.vox.com/even-better/23144784/why-rituals-not-routine

OECD. (2017). Students' sense of belonging at school and their relations with teachers. In *PISA 2015 Results (Volume III): Students' Well-Being* (pp. 117–131). OECD. https://doi.org/10.1787/9789264273856-11-en

Panorama Education. (n.d.). Panorama Education student survey: Sense of belonging. https://go.panoramaed.com/hubfs/Panorama-Education_Student-Survey_Sense%20of%20Belonging.pdf?hsLang=en

Pierson, R. F. (Director). (2013, May). Every kid needs a champion. www.ted.com/talks/rita_pierson_every_kid_needs_a_champion

Pietrafetta, M. (n.d.). Reciprocal relationships and empathy. *Academic Approach.* www.academicapproach.com/reciprocal-relationships-empathy/

Ryan, R. M., & Deci, E. L. (2000). Intrinsic and extrinsic motivations: Classic definitions and new directions. *Contemporary Educational Psychology, 25*(1), 54–67. https://doi.org/10.1006/ceps.1999.1020

Sethi, J., & Scales, P. C. (2020). Developmental relationships and school success: How teachers, parents, and friends affect educational outcomes and what actions students say matter most. *Contemporary Educational Psychology, 63*, 101904. https://doi.org/10.1016/j.cedpsych.2020.101904

Seton, H. (2021, January 8). A daily ritual that builds trust and community among students. *Edutopia.* www.edutopia.org/article/daily-ritual-builds-trust-and-community-among-students

Sparks, S. D. (2019, March 12). Why teacher–student relationships matter. *Education Week.* www.edweek.org/teaching-learning/why-teacher–student-relationships-matter/2019/03

Staffen, W., Kronbichler, M., Aichhorn, M., Mair, A., & Ladurner, G. (2006). Selective brain activity in response to one's own name in the persistent vegetative state. *Journal of Neurology, Neurosurgery & Psychiatry, 77*(12), 1383–1384. https://doi.org/10.1136/jnnp.2006.095166

Theisen-Homer, V. (2021). Preparing teachers for relationships with students: Two visions, two approaches.

Journal of Teacher Education, 72(3), 271–283. https://doi.org/10.1177/0022487120922223

University of Eastern Finland. (2015, November 3). Empathetic teachers enhance children's motivation for learning. *ScienceDaily*. www.sciencedaily.com/releases/2015/11/151103064738.htm

Van Ryzin, M. J., & Roseth, C. J. (2019). Cooperative learning effects on peer relations and alcohol use in middle school. *Journal of Applied Developmental Psychology*, 64, 101059. https://doi.org/10.1016/j.appdev.2019.101059

Van Ryzin, M. J., Roseth, C. J., & Biglan, A. (2020). Mediators of effects of cooperative learning on prosocial behavior in middle school. *International Journal of Applied Positive Psychology*, 5(1–2), 37–52. https://doi.org/10.1007/s41042-020-00026-8

Van Ryzin, M. J., Roseth, C. J., & McClure, H. (2020). The effects of cooperative learning on peer relations, academic support, and engagement in learning among students of color. *The Journal of Educational Research*, 113(4), 283–291. https://doi.org/10.1080/00220671.2020.1806016

Wang, E. L., & Lee, E. (2019). The use of responsive circles in schools: An exploratory study. *Journal of Positive Behavior Interventions*, 21(3), 181–194. https://doi.org/10.1177/1098300718793428

Wentzel, K. R. (1998). Social relationships and motivation in middle school: The role of parents, teachers, and peers. *Journal of Educational Psychology*, 90(2), 202–209. https://doi.org/10.1037/0022-0663.90.2.202

Xie, K., Vongkulluksn, V. W., Cheng, S.-L., & Jiang, Z. (2022). Examining high-school students' motivation change through a person-centered approach. *Journal of Educational Psychology*, 114(1), 89–107. https://doi.org/10.1037/edu0000507

Zhao, D., Rutledge Simmons, D., & Duva, M. (2019). *Measuring students' class-level sense of belonging: A social-network-based approach.* American Society for Engineering Education, Tampa, FL. https://peer.asee.org/measuring-students-class-level-sense-of-belonging-a-social-network-based-approach.pdf

What Is "Relevance" and Why Is it Important?

Self-Determination Theory, which may be the mostly widely known theory on human motivation, was originally developed by Professors Richard Ryan and Edward Deci (2000), and highlights the topics of the first three chapters of this book—autonomy, competence and relatedness. Many researchers also either include "relevance" within the "autonomy" category (Assor et al., 2002) or explicitly add it as a fourth criteria (Center on Education Policy, 2012).

The French word "relevant" originally meant "helpful" (Online Etymology Dictionary, 2021) and that's what relevance means today in the context of intrinsic motivation—do students see what they are being taught as useful to them in their present lives and/or will it help them achieve their future goals? In addition, the word "relevance" can apply to topics or activities of "interest" to them, even if they may not necessarily be considered "helpful" or "useful" (Center on Education Policy, 2012, p. 4). For example, I found an article I recently read about door-to-door salespeople "interesting," but nothing in it is particularly "useful" to me.

Personal relevance has been found to be a "particularly important" predictor of student engagement

 DOI: 10.4324/9781315208824-5

(Assor et al., 2002, p. 261; Romero, 2019) especially for students who might feel less confident in their academic skills ((Lazowski & Hulleman, 2016).

Unfortunately, according to the very limited data available, about half of students don't feel that what they are learning in class right now is very relevant to what they do and will be doing outside of school (Stringer, 2017). A recent survey of educators found that they felt that students not seeing relevance in coursework was one of the biggest motivational challenges they faced as teachers in the classroom (Hulleman & Barron, 2013).

If studies are concluding that it's important for students to feel that school content is relevant to their lives; if many students might be saying that they don't feel like it is; and if teachers are agreeing that students don't appear to see what is happening in school as relevant, then perhaps it would be worth us reflecting on what we've been doing in the classroom and consider making some changes . . .

What Are Ways Teachers Can Ensure that Students Feel that the Classroom Is Relevant to Their Lives?

Doing many of the activities in previous chapters can also contribute to students feeling like classes are relevant to their lives. Here are a few more (not necessarily listed in any order of preference or effectiveness).

42. Students "Self-Generating" Connections

"Self-generation" is the term used to describe having students themselves identify how what they are learning can be relevant to their lives and goals (Albrecht & Karabenick, 2018).

What Is "Relevance" and Why Is it Important?

There are at least two different ways to approach this kind of "self-generation." One is being more directive in asking students to connect a specific lesson to their lives, and the other is having them choose any school content and describe how it is relevant to them.

An example of the first strategy was demonstrated by researchers who had students write a paragraph after a lesson explaining how they thought what they had learned would be useful to their lives. Writing one to eight of these during a semester led to positive learning gains, especially for those students who had previously been "low performers" (Hulleman & Harackiewicz, 2009).

This successful experiment prompted the University of Pennsylvania's Character Lab (co-founded by Angela Duckworth) to create a specific "Build Connections" lesson (Character Lab, 2018) using the second form of "self-generation"—having students consider a variety of topics they had learned about in school and making a connection to one or more of them. In the lesson and materials, including scaffolded student forms, that are freely available to teachers and students (see the EdTech Toolbox for the link), students make one list of their interests and goals, then right next to it a list of topics they have learned about in class. They are then asked to make lines connecting as many of the two different lists as possible. Finally, they choose one from each column and explain in a short paragraph how they are connected.

The New York Times Learning Network also had an annual contest for three years inviting students to submit essays making similar connections (see the EdTech Toolbox for the links).

Depending on the class, this is the scaffolded sequence I usually follow to assist students "self-generate" these connections:

1. I begin by having students only use the Character Lab's "Build Connections" forms every other week for a month-or-two, though I will also use it periodically throughout the entire year.
2. After students become familiar with the activity, I'll share some student-written winners from *The New York Times* Learning Network contest (there are many to choose from). They are slightly more detailed than the writing expected in the "Build Connections" lesson. I then ask that when we do this activity in the future, I would appreciate their trying to use those responses as models.
3. Then, throughout the year, I'll periodically either use the "Build Connections" lesson or specifically ask students to write about a particular activity that we have just completed.

This process has worked well, and students often comment in anonymous class evaluations that they like doing it. Several, in fact, have told me that the activities helped instill in them a discipline where they almost automatically ask themselves how to connect to every lesson.

Of course, an essential prerequisite for making these self-generated connections a successful activity is that we have to make sure the lessons we teach are, indeed, relevant to our students' lives. We need to know our students, and we may need to be prepared to modify our curriculum.

EDTECH TOOLBOX

For links to the Character Lab lesson plan, The New York Times Learning Network's essay examples, and other related resources, go to "The Best Ideas for Helping Students Connect Lessons to Their Interests & the World" (https://larryferlazzo.edublogs.org/2017/12/09/the-best-ideas-for-helping-students-connect-lessons-to-their-interests-the-world/).

43. "Direct Communication" from Teacher-to-Student about Connections

As opposed to students "self-generating" how class content is connected to their lives, "direct communication" simply means teachers explaining how it's relevant. Some researchers have found that, though this method might be effective with students who perceive themselves as well-skilled academically, it may actually be de-motivating for others for various reasons (Hulleman et al., 2010). Some contributing factors could be because it may be viewed as a condescending message (Denworth, 2021), and/or they may want to reassert autonomy (Yeager et al., 2014a).

Other research, however, suggests that teachers pointing out connections is better than not discussing them at all (Sparks, 2013), especially if those connections are more near-term (the math we're learning will help you figure out how to get the best car loan) than far-term (the math we're learning will help you purchase a house (Priniski et al., 2018).

In education circles, a common question that is asked when discussing a classroom activity is, "Who is doing the thinking?" There is little question, or no question at all, that students "self-generating" their connections is the better strategy to pursue. However, we have a finite amount of time with our students and, given that challenge, I sometimes just tell students the connection. The real question is "Which do we tend to do more of: self-generation or direct communication?"

It's important to note that I also sometimes use a method to highlight relevance that could be described as "in between" "self-generation" and "direct communication." These lessons use the idea of "guided self-discovery" that is also found in inductive learning (described in earlier chapters) where a teacher prepares materials and questions designed to "nudge" students along a certain path.

An example of this kind of lesson designed to promote the relevance of improving literacy skills can be found in the "Our World of Text" lesson plan in my previous book, *Self-Driven Learning* (Ferlazzo, 2013, p. 152). The student hand-outs for that lesson can be freely downloaded at the book's website (www.routledge.com/Self-Driven-Learning-Teaching-Strategies-for-Student-Motivation/Ferlazzo/p/book/9781596672390). Among other activities, that lesson shares a list of potential kinds of outside-of-school writing tasks (correspondence, notes, reports, etc.) and asks students to develop potential scenarios when they might be required to perform them. They also apply the same process to potential texts they might need to read (training manuals, instructions, etc.) and do the same with them.

In these lessons, and in similar others any teacher can develop, students are provided limited guidance to develop their own understandings of how what they are learning in school can be relevant to their lives.

44. Helping Students Develop a Purpose for Learning

When I was a community organizer, our "bread-and-butter" was identifying people's immediate self-interests—getting local roads repaired, more affordable neighborhood childcare, etc.—and working with them to get those problems resolved. The hardest-working, and most effective, volunteer leaders—the ones who spent hours upon hours having individual meetings with neighbors and making phone calls—tended to be people who also had a second and broader self-interest beyond the immediate problem that affected them. These leaders explicitly viewed fixing the individual problem as a step along the way towards making the community better for everyone.

In a similar way, many of our students' self-interests may also be immediate—the relevance of a writing lesson to a student might be helping them write a better resume to get a job. But our students' self-interests may also be broader—what researchers call a *purpose for learning*—a goal of benefiting oneself but also contributing in some way to the greater good (Yeager et al., 2014a). These are students who might say something like "I want to be an engineer because I like math and I want to help create something that might help the community."

In the classroom, just as in the community organizing context, people can be engaged and motivated to act on "self-oriented motives" (Yeager et al., 2014a, p. 560). But just as organizers have found that those who also have a broader vision are more committed to action, researchers have found that students who also have what researchers call "self-transcendent motives" demonstrate higher classroom engagement and motivation, increased persistence when tasks might not be as interesting, and deeper learning.

Some of our students, like some neighborhood residents during community organizing campaigns, might already have this kind of "purpose," though studies suggest it might be a very small percentage of them (Wallis, 2018). How do we foster its development in others? In community organizing, it takes a thoughtful strategic effort by the organizer to help make it happen. In the classroom, researchers have found it might take a similarly targeted plan by teachers to help some students consider expanding their definition of what they consider relevant to them.

The goal is not to tell students what making the world a better place should look like to them. Rather, the goal is to encourage students to consider if making the world a better place is important to them and, if so, how learning in school might help them make that happen.

In a study, researchers were successful in achieving this goal by first asking students for ideas on how to make the world a better place, then sharing statistics showing that many young people were motivated to work hard in school to help themselves and to help make a better world. Next, students read short paragraphs by older students sharing similar reasons for learning in school. Finally, students were asked to write their own paragraphs about their education goals for younger people to read (Yeager et al., 2014a).

You could certainly replicate this procedure and, in fact, the researchers have made most of their materials freely available online (Yeager et al., 2014b).

Personally, I've used a more simple strategy that, though it has not been rigorously evaluated, seems to at least touch on similar themes and, based on anonymous student evaluations, may have similar impacts.

Dr. Martin Luther King, Jr. wrote a short essay in 1947 when he was in college titled "The Purpose of Education." Though I have had students read it in the past, more recently I have them read a piece by educator Candace Obadina (2018) that's available online, titled "Reflection on MLK's Paper, The Purpose of Education." Ms. Obadina does an excellent job highlighting the most important parts of the essay in a very accessible way. She is writing for an audience of teachers, but students can gain an equal amount from reading it.

After reading her commentary, I ask students to create a short slideshow (writing a short essay response can also be an option) responding to this prompt:

> According to Ms. Candace Obadina, what does Dr. Martin Luther King, Jr. believe to be the purpose or purposes of education? Do you agree or disagree that education has those purposes and why? What is your purpose for learning in school?

I give students the option of working with partners, as long as they respond to the last part of the prompt individually.

Students share their slideshows in small groups or in a "speed-dating" style, and we then discuss them as a class. Many, if not most, students write some version that their purpose for learning is both to improve themselves and to improve the world. With luck, at least some of my students are then more likely to have a broader definition of how school can be "relevant" to their lives.

45. Connecting to Student Prior Knowledge

During my community organizing career, our primary strategy was to learn people's stories, have them share those stories with others, and then help them develop a new interpretation of those stories. This new interpretation then was the engine that would propel themselves to action. It's similar to a challenge we face in the classroom—we need to help students connect our lesson content to their background knowledge and then attach new understandings and learnings to it. Some examples could be connecting (Ferlazzo, 2015, p. 17):

- Their lives to the study of Mount Everest by reflecting on what its first blind summitter meant when he said, "There are summits everywhere . . . you just have to know where to look" and then having students share their own "summits."
- Their experiences during the COVID epidemic to what happened during the Spanish Flu.
- What they've seen and/or done on social media with information literacy strategies.
- Stories of important women in their lives to learning about important women in history and finding the commonalities between them.
- Their experiences of using the scientific method to successfully learn anything (cooking, playing basketball) to its use in the scientific process.

46. Cultivate the "Curiosity Gap"

As explained in the first part of this chapter, "relevance" can also be used to describe student interest in a topic. "Curiosity" is often used interchangeably with "interest," but researchers have recently considered how to distinguish the two from each other. A gap in knowledge, particularly when there is a low-level of knowledge about the topic is generally the trigger for curiosity. Interest can be present when there is either a low or high level of knowledge. Finally, the goal of curiosity is to fill in the "gap," while the goal of interest is enjoyment, often through the acquisition of more knowledge (Tang et al., 2020). In addition to promoting intrinsic motivation (Pluck & Johnson, 2011), high levels of curiosity have also increased academic success (von Stumm et al., 2011).

What are ways we can cultivate what is sometimes called the "curiosity gap" (Dean, 2022) so that students' eagerness to fill it in makes our class content feel more "relevant" to them? Strategies discussed earlier in this book, including Problem-Based Learning (where students have to choose a problem to solve) and concept attainment (where they have to solve a "puzzle" to identify why some exemplars are under "yes" and others under "no"), can cultivate curiosity. Here are a few more:

One way is to introduce a topic, theme or chapter, invite students to co-create a list of questions they have about it or things they would like to know about it, and then make sure those questions are answered in lessons—either by you or, even better, by students "doing the thinking," finding the answers, and then sharing them with the class (Freberg, 2020).

Studies have also found that introducing "controversial" issues tends to whet student curiosity (Goodwin, 2014). What school subject doesn't have a plethora of controversies or, at least content that can be framed as controversial?

Education researcher Dylan Wiliam recommends "making feedback into detective work" (Howell, 2022; Marshall, 2016). In other words, instead of telling a student, "Your second claim needs more evidence to support it," we would say to the student, "One of your claims needs more evidence—try to identify which one it is, add more evidence, and show me what you've come up with."

47. Engage with Problems in the Community

Previous chapters have discussed small student groups participating in Problem-Based Learning activities, which can include—though are not limited to—issues facing local communities. Students participating in an active role improving their communities can increase motivation by connecting to "relevance," and studies have shown that teenage "activists" tend to have better academic performance and better long-term financial outcomes than those who are not involved in these types of activities (Damour, 2018).

Another way of approaching this idea is having the entire class choose one community problem to focus on. Links to a variety of detailed plans to implement this kind of "unit" can be found in the EdTech Toolbox, as well as in one of my previous books, *English Language Learners: Teaching Strategies That Work* (Ferlazzo, 2010, p. 44).

The primary process I've used for these kinds of non-partisan classwide projects is to first have students in the class interview each other, and family and community members, to ask what community problems concern them the most. Students report back, and then we make a list of the top priorities. Next, small groups turn these typically big "problems" that made the list, like crime, lack of jobs, and immigration, into small actionable "issues" that are specific and achievable in a short time. For example, the problem of "lack of jobs" can be turned into "Asking our City Councilperson to assign a staffperson to work with us on developing a summer jobs program for youth." Finally, students decide to take action on one of these issues.

In past years, my classes have used this process to organize:

- A job training "fair" at school where representatives of multiple job training organizations and agencies made brief presentations to a joint student and community assembly, and then set-up tables where people could find more information.
- A question-and-answer panel with immigration attorneys, again for both students and their families.
- A multilingual campaign to encourage neighborhood residents to complete U.S. Census forms.

EDTECH TOOLBOX

More ideas, along with detailed lesson plans, on class engagement with community problems can be found at "The 'Best' Ideas for Students & Classes to Be Engaged in Community Improvement Projects—Please Contribute More Ideas!" (https://larryferlazzo.edublogs.org/2022/08/04/the-best-ideas-for-students-classes-to-be-engaged-in-community-improvement-projects-please-contribute-more-ideas/).

48. Hyper-Personalize Learning

"Personalized learning" has become a bit of a "buzzword" in education circles, and more often than not is used to describe adaptive software that modifies itself to the individual student's answers to problems and questions (Herold, 2019). However, a recent university experiment where a science class had students examine the microbial bodies found on their own body to teach microbiome analysis brings the term to an entirely different level! Student engagement and motivation in that science class substantially increased as a result of this innovation (Weber et al., 2018).

Teachers in any subject can apply this idea to their class. For example, I have had students study—and make presentations about—the origins of their names, characteristics of their neighborhoods, and the attributes of their home cultures. Other classes could have students analyze the various costs and benefits of how they travel to-and-from-school, as well as their diets. There are a variety of topics that are hyper personal and relevant that can be used in standards-based and rigorous lessons.

49. Promote "Education-Dependent Future Identities"

Researchers have found that promoting "education-dependent future identities" to students results in increased student academic motivation (Destin & Oyserman, 2010). Just showing students charts—and reading the data aloud—that compare adult income by educational level attainment resulted in better grades over time. These statistics show higher incomes for people who go to college over only high school graduates, and increased salaries for every additional year of college completion. Links to resources to share with students can be found in the EdTech Toolbox.

I do this quick activity every year and I also sometimes post the charts on a classroom wall and leave them there, at least for a while. I think it's important to also explicitly point out that there is nothing "wrong" with not going to college and that, yes, there are exceptions to this data. I present the information in the spirit that these are important facts for students to know, and that they can do with it what they will.

> **EDTECH TOOLBOX**
>
> Find accessible charts and infographics on income according to educational attainment level at "The Best Resources for Showing Students Why They Should Continue Their Academic Career" (https://larryferlazzo.edublogs.org/2010/02/24/the-best-resources-for-showing-students-why-they-should-continue-their-academic-career/).

50. Playing Games

On the surface, even though playing a competitive game can certainly fit into the "relevance" category because many students would find it interesting, it might also appear to cater to extrinsic motivation, not the intrinsic kind. Indeed, the research is decidedly mixed on the question (Dahlstrøm, 2003). However, studies have also found that there are certain ways that teachers can "tilt" game-playing in the intrinsic direction.

Much of the research on motivation has focused on the negative impact of "tangible" rewards—physical objects, desired activities, or something else that has a real impact on a person's life. On the other hand, some researchers suggest that if game points and levels don't mean anything outside of the game environment, then these "intangible" rewards are unlikely to damage intrinsic motivation (Dahlstrøm, 2003).

Though research may not be definitive about the impact of games on intrinsic motivation, here are some recommendations (some based on research, others based on my own teaching experience) on how to maximize the odds that playing games in your classroom can not only enhance learning, but also help create the conditions for students' intrinsic motivation to grow:

- Make the game very low-stakes, or no-stakes at all. Whether it's a classroom game where students are using physical mini-whiteboards, or an online one where students are playing on their devices, make the intangible reward the excitement of the game itself! Of course, I am not above giving out a small package of fruit snacks to first, second and third place finishers. If you are going to give a tangible reward, give a similar one that increases the fun (in my experience, students almost always share their "winnings") and is a "by-product" of winning, not its purpose.
- To maximize students' sense of relatedness and to increase the chances of as many students "winning" as possible, have students play in small (two-four students each) teams as much as possible, rather than alone. Sometimes have students choose their own, and at other times the teacher determines them.
- Don't be afraid to manipulate a game. For example, if students are playing an online game and I'll see a student who is at the top of the leader board who usually isn't there, I'll "accidentally" end the game so he/she can win.

- To ensure that games function as both a formative assessment and an opportunity to enhance students' sense of competence, make sure the questions cover topics that have been previously taught in class.
- To enhance students' sense of autonomy, create opportunities for students to make their own games and play them as a class (remember the question, "Who is doing the thinking?"). For example, I often have students create an online game as part of small group oral presentations. They present to the class, and then the audience plays a game answering questions based on the presentation they just heard.

EDTECH TOOLBOX

Visit "'Best' Lists of the Week: Learning Games" (https://larryferlazzo.edublogs.org/2018/03/05/best-lists-of-the-week-online-learning-games/) to find hundreds of ideas for in-classroom and online games and how to play/create them.

What Questions Can Teachers Ask Themselves to Ensure that Their Strategies to Promote Relevance in the Classroom Are Also Culturally Responsive?

- Am I carefully reviewing what "self-generated" connections students are saying—or not saying—they are making to my lessons? If the connections appear weak or non-existent, am I reviewing my curriculum to consider making modifications to ensure that it is racially and ethnically inclusive, substantive and engaging to increase the odds of students viewing our class as relevant?

- Even though I have many students in my classes, am I making it a priority to learn about their personal interests and goals through having conversations and creating opportunities where students can express them in writing? Do I take the time to review them in some kind of systematic way? If some of my students' primary languages are ones I don't speak, do I seek assistance from a school translator or at least use a tool like Google Translate?

- As I learn about my students' personal interests and goals, am I acknowledging and respecting ones that might be representative of different cultures? Am I taking time to learn about ones unfamiliar to me so I can consider ways to connect them to my lessons?

- Do I try to stay aware of "serious" current events and "pop culture" news that might be on the minds of my students so I can be alert to lesson connections? It could be a matter of just once-a-week asking a student what their classmates are talking about or what's on their mind and having a conversation for a minute-or-two.

- Do I genuinely encourage students to become active citizens and create opportunities for them to choose to take action to improve their communities? If I do, do I steer students towards "safe" topics that would be less "controversial"? Am I overly cautious about parental and administrator "pushback" and try to put those student passions on the "backburner?" Are there actions I can take to obtain parental and administrator "buy-in," like having pre-conversations explaining how these activities are Standards-based, academically rigorous, and pedagogically sound?

- Am I careful when making connections to students' prior knowledge that I am not aggravating

173

their trauma? For example, during a time when news outlets were highlighting heavy migration from Central America because of gang violence, I privately asked students from there who were in my class how they would feel about our discussing the reasons for the exodus and made it very clear that we wouldn't do the lesson if they felt it would be too hard for them to experience it. Eagerness to do the lesson, as well as sadness about the situation, was their primary response as each showed me photos of their friends who had been murdered. I honored their openness and said that they could leave the room at any time during the lesson and go next door (I would make arrangements with the other teacher). It turned out to be an extraordinarily powerful lesson because of their participation, and one student did make the decision to leave in the middle of it (though, he nevertheless thanked me for doing the lesson).

- Education researcher Carol Dweck says, "Every student can help you become a better teacher" (McKibben, 2019). Am I genuinely open to learning from my students about how I can improve as an educator?

- Do I create equal opportunities for English Language Learners and others to make learning relevant to them by ensuring my content is as accessible as possible through strategies like "engineering" texts we use in class (making changes to texts like creating more white space, bold headings, and including vocabulary definitions) and not speaking too fast, along with other language scaffolds discussed earlier in this book? And that I'm making a similar strong effort to do the same with any assessments I use? See the EdTech

Toolbox for resources on how to "engineer" text and use other strategies to support ELLs in classes.

- One way to increase the odds of students finding school content relevant is by being conscious of what writer Chimamanda Ngozi Adichie describes in her popular TED Talk as "the dangers of a single story" available at www.ted.com/talks/ chimamanda_ngozi_adichie_the_danger_of_a_ single_story. Do I look at the textbooks and the curriculum that we use and do an "audit" to identify whose stories might be left out of them? See the EdTech Toolbox for resources that could be helpful in this process.

EDTECH TOOLBOX

Learn ways to make your class texts more accessible at "The Best Strategies for 'Engineering' Text so That it's More Accessible to ELLs" (https:// larryferlazzo.edublogs.org/2022/02/16/the-best-strategies-for-engineering-text-so-that-its-more-accessible-to-ells/).

Find more ways to support English Language Learners in your classes at "The Best Advice To Content Teachers About Supporting English Language Learners" https://larryferlazzo.edub logs.org/2017/09/08/the-best-advice-to-content-teachers-about-supporting-english-language-learners/.

See "The Best Resources on 'The Danger of a Single Story'" https://larryferlazzo.edublogs.org/ 2016/12/20/the-best-resources-on-the-danger-of-a-single-story/ for strategies on how to guard against that danger in the classroom.

References

Albrecht, J. R., & Karabenick, S. A. (2018). Relevance for learning and motivation in education. *The Journal of Experimental Education, 86*(1), 1–10. https://doi.org/10.1080/00220973.2017.1380593

Assor, A., Kaplan, H., & Roth, G. (2002). Choice is good, but relevance is excellent: Autonomy-enhancing and suppressing teacher behaviours predicting students' engagement in schoolwork. *British Journal of Educational Psychology, 72*(2), 261–278. https://doi.org/10.1348/000709902158883

Center on Education Policy. (2012). What is motivation and why does it matter? The George Washington University. https://files.eric.ed.gov/fulltext/ED532670.pdf

Character Lab. (2018). Build connections for classrooms: Overview. https://characterlab.org/activities/build-connections-for-classrooms/

Dahlstrøm, C. (2003). Impacts of gamification on intrinsic motivation. www.ntnu.edu/documents/139799/12791499 90/04+Article+Final_camildah_fors%C3%B8k_2017-12-06-13-53-55_TPD4505.Camilla.Dahlstr%C3%B8m.pdf

Damour, L. (2018, March 12). Why demonstrating is good for kids. *The New York Times.* www.nytimes.com/2018/03/12/well/family/why-demonstrating-is-good-for-kids.html

Dean, J. (2022, March 25). How to use the curiosity gap to motivate change. *PsyBlog.* www.spring.org.uk/2022/03/emotion-change.php

Denworth, L. (2021). Adolescent brains are wired to want status and respect: That's an opportunity for teachers and parents. *Scientific American.* www.scientificamerican.com/article/adolescent-brains-are-wired-to-want-status-and-respect-thats-an-opportunity-for-teachers-and-parents/

Destin, M., & Oyserman, D. (2010). Incentivizing education: Seeing schoolwork as an investment, not a chore. *Journal of Experimental Social Psychology, 46*(5), 846–849. https://doi.org/10.1016/j.jesp.2010.04.004

Ferlazzo, L. (2010). *English language learners: Teaching strategies that work.* Linworth.

Ferlazzo, L. (2013). *Self-driven learning: Teaching strategies for student motivation.* Eye on Education.

Ferlazzo, L. (2015). *Building a community of self-motivated learners: Strategies to help students thrive in school and beyond.* Routledge.

Freberg, L. (2020, June 19). Using curiosity gaps to enhance student engagement. https://teachpsych.org/page-1784686/9048187

Goodwin, B. (2014). Curiosity is fleeting, but teachable. *Education Leadership, 72*(1). www.ascd.org/el/articles/curiosity-is-fleeting-but-teachable

Herold, B. (2019, November 5). What is personalized learning? *Education Week.* www.edweek.org/technology/what-is-personalized-learning/2019/11

Howell, J. (2022, February 19). Another pearl of wisdom from @dylanwiliam: Feedback should be detective work, not information. What a great way to engage students. https://twitter.com/jk_howell/status/149521043145505177

Hulleman, C., & Barron, K. (2013, April 27). *Teacher perceptions of student motivational challenges and best strategies to enhance motivation.* American Educational Research Association, San Francisco, California.

Hulleman, C. S., Godes, O., Hendricks, B. L., & Harackiewicz, J. M. (2010). Enhancing interest and performance with a utility value intervention. *Journal of Educational Psychology, 102*(4), 880–895. https://doi.org/10.1037/a0019506

Hulleman, C. S., & Harackiewicz, J. M. (2009). Promoting interest and performance in high school science classes. *Science, 326*(5958), 1410–1412. https://doi.org/10.1126/science.1177067

Lazowski, R. A., & Hulleman, C. S. (2016). Motivation interventions in education: A meta-analytic review. *Review of Educational Research, 86*(2), 602–640. https://doi.org/10.3102/0034654315617832

Marshall, K. (2016, April 5). Dylan Wiliam on feedback that makes a difference to students. *The Marshall Memo.* www.tieonline.com/article/1836/dylan-wiliam-on-feedback-that-makes-a-difference-to-students

McKibben, S. (2019). Carol Dweck on fixed mindsets in new teachers. *Education Leadership, 77*(1).

www.ascd.org/el/articles/carol-dweck-on-fixed-mindsets-in-new-teachers

Obadina, C. (2018, April 3). Reflection on MLK's paper, "the purpose of education." *Memphis Teacherr Residency.* https://memphistr.org/reflection-on-mlks-paper-the-purpose-of-education/

Online Etymology Dictionary. (2021, June 23). Relevant (adj.). www.etymonline.com/word/relevant?ref=etymonline_crossreference

Pluck, G., & Johnson, H. (2011). Stimulating curiosity to enhance learning. *GESJ: Education Science and Psychology, 2*(19).

Priniski, S. J., Hecht, C. A., & Harackiewicz, J. M. (2018). Making learning personally meaningful: A new framework for relevance research. *The Journal of Experimental Education, 86*(1), 11–29. https://doi.org/10.1080/00220973.2017.1380589

Romero, C. (2019). *What we know about purpose & relevance from scientific research.* The Mindset Scholars Network. https://studentexperiencenetwork.org/wp-content/uploads/2015/09/What-We-Know-About-Purpose-and-Relevance-.pdf

Ryan, R. M., & Deci, E. L. (2000). Self-determination theory and the facilitation of intrinsic motivation, social development, and well-being. *American Psychologist, 55*(1), 68–78. https://doi.org/10.1037/0003-066X.55.1.68

Sparks, S. D. (2013, July 10). "Active" student engagement goes beyond class behavior, study finds. *Education Week.* www.edweek.org/education/active-student-engagement-goes-beyond-class-behavior-study-finds/2013/07

Stringer, K. (2017, December 11). Only half of students think what they're learning in school is relevant to the real world, survey says. *The74.* www.the74million.org/article/only-half-of-students-think-what-theyre-learning-in-school-is-relevant-to-the-real-world-survey-says

Tang, X., Renninger, A., Hidi, S., Murayama, K., Lavonen, J., & Salmela-Aro, K. (2020). The differences and similarities between curiosity and interest: Meta-analysis and network analyses [Preprint]. PsyArXiv. https://doi.org/10.31234/osf.io/wfprn

von Stumm, S., Hell, B., & Chamorro-Premuzic, T. (2011). The hungry mind: Intellectual curiosity is the third pillar of academic performance. *Perspectives on Psychological Science*, 6(6), 574–588. https://doi.org/10.1177/1745691 611421204

Wallis, C. (2018, January 3). The benefits of helping teens identify their purpose in life. *Mind/Shift*. www. kqed.org/mindshift/49937/the-benefits-of-helping-teens-identify-purpose-in-life

Weber, K. S., Bridgewater, L. C., Jensen, J. L., Breakwell, D. P., Nielsen, B. L., & Johnson, S. M. (2018). Personal microbiome analysis improves student engagement and interest in Immunology, Molecular Biology, and Genomics undergraduate courses. *PLOS ONE*, 13(4), e0193696. https://doi.org/10.1371/journal.pone.0193696

Yeager, D. S., Henderson, M. D., Paunesku, D., Walton, G., D'Mello, S., Spitzer, B., & Duckworth, A. L. (2014a). Boring but important: A self-transcendent purpose for learning fosters academic self-regulation. *Journal of Personality and Social Psychology*, 107(4), 559–580. https://doi.org/10.1037/a0037637.supp

Yeager, D. S., Henderson, M. D., Paunesku, D., Walton, G., D'Mello, S., Spitzer, B., & Duckworth, A. L. (2014b). Supplemental material for "Boring but important: A self-transcendent purpose for learning fosters academic self-regulation." *Journal of Personality and Social Psychology*, 107(4), 559–580. https://doi.org/10.1037/a0037637.supp

Afterword

I've often shared this story of the time I lived in an elevated house, on the bottom of a small hill. It had a storm drain on the street in front of it. During the summer, I would pour wood chips in the small dirt area between the sidewalk and the curb, and during heavy winter rainstorms the drain would get clogged up with debris floating downhill. Water would go over the curb, and all the wood chips would float away, leaving a muddy area. Each year my wife would strongly suggest I plant grass or bushes in that area so that it could withstand the water, and each year I instead chose the short-term solution of wood chips. It appeared easier to me and seemed to work most of the time—until the bad weather hit. I chose this solution even though planting grass and bushes would have saved me time and money over the long-term, made the neighborhood look better and, in fact, would have probably attacked the cause of the problem by reducing the amount of debris that was clogging the drain. I had other things on my "to do" list that I felt were more important and was more comfortable with a problem I was familiar with than with a solution that was new to me—having a "green thumb" was not on my resume.

Let's see how we can get rid of the wood chips of extrinsic motivation. Instead, let's plant some nice grass and bushes, and create the conditions in which they can grow well . . .